INTENTIONALITY
Live on Purpose!

Wendy K. Walters

INTENTIONALITY
Live on Purpose!

Editor: Dr. Philip R. Byler | www.thephantomscribe.com

Photos (Back Cover, About the Author): Charity Bradshaw

Printed in the USA

ISBN: 978-0-9857942-2-4

Prepared for Publication By

PALM TREE
PUBLICATIONS

Palm Tree Publications is a Division of Palm Tree Productions
www.palmtreeproductions.com
PO BOX 122 | KELLER, TX | 76244

Scripture references appear in the endnotes:

Scripture taken from the Amplified® Bible, Copyright © 1954, 1958, 1962, 1964, 1965, 1987 by The Lockman Foundation. La Habra, CA. Used by permission.

Scripture taken from the King James Version of the Bible ®, Copyright © 1982 by Broadman & Holman Publishers, Nashville, TN. Used by permission. All rights reserved.

Scripture taken from The Message ®. Copyright © 1993, 1994, 1995, 1996, 2000, 2001, 2002. Used by permission of NavPress Publishing Group. Colorado Springs, CO. All rights reserved.

Scripture taken from the HOLY BIBLE, NEW INTERNATIONAL VERSION ®. Copyright © 1973, 1978, 1984 Biblica. Used by permission of Zondervan. All rights reserved.

Scripture taken from the New King James Version (NKJV) of the Bible. Copyright © 1982 by Thomas Nelson, Inc. Used by permission. All rights reserved.

To Contact the Author:

www.wendykwalters.com

www.palmtreeproductions.com

"Wendy Walters has an amazing gift to call out the passions and purpose in other people. More than that—she can teach you to empower yourself. Reading *Intentionality—Live on Purpose!* is like sitting down with this powerhouse of a woman for a one-on-one coaching session. In just a short time, she will lead you to overcome self-doubt, leap over thoughts of mediocrity, and make a quality decision to live on purpose."

Jan Greenwood
Pastor of PINK (Gateway Women)
www.gatewaypeople.com

"This is a stimulating read filled with practical application. As I turned the pages, it felt like I was having a conversation with Wendy, receiving pointers on how to get out of the "ditch." I was ready to not only leap out of bed, but ready to burn my ships and go conquer Mexico!

Intentionality is dynamic, designed activity, and intentional neglect is a great concept ... wow! This is a book for men and women, young and old—for anyone who has had it with "ditch life" and wants to live filled with passion, purpose, and intention."

John R. "Barney" Barnes, CDR USN (Ret.)
Author of *Born to Be A Warrior*

CONTENTS

BECOME INTENTIONAL.
YOU HAVE THE OPPORTUNITY TO
CRAFT YOUR DESTINY AND STEP
INTO YOUR UNLIMITED FUTURE.

CHAPTER ONE

INTENTIONAL DESIGN

Most of us understand the value of vision. We recognize that people with blindness must overcome a great handicap to interact with the world in ways the rest of us take for granted. If you don't believe me, try closing your eyes or wearing a mask for a few hours. Now, without the assistance of your vision, how well do you function? Can you work? Can you drive? Can you even walk around a room without injuring yourself or someone else?

Vision is important.

Chances are, you (or someone you love) requires the aid of glasses or contact lenses to be fully functional in a seeing world. Without them, their quality of life would surely suffer. If you can't see clearly, it is difficult to be fully engaged in your world. Even having a conversation with someone can become a challenge if you are unable to see facial expressions or read body language.

When someone's natural vision is impaired, the use of a properly prescribed lens to bring the world into focus is vital. I know. Without corrective lenses, my vision is reduced to counting blurry blobs which are supposed to be fingers, just a few feet away from me. I can't even recognize my loved ones by their faces; they have to speak before I know who I'm talking to.

When I am in a familiar environment, I can function well enough, even without my glasses. Inside my own home, I can walk around at full speed, find my way to the bathroom, or pour a glass of water without a spill. I can actually walk around in complete darkness without needing to turn on a light. I know my way around so well I can function even though I can't see.

However, put me in a hotel room and I am paralyzed without my glasses. I won't take two steps away from the bed without them. When the security of familiarity is removed, the restrictions caused by my inability to see clearly are highlighted. When I am in a well-known environment, I can fake it; if a stranger were present to witness me walk around, they would not know I couldn't see. If I were dropped off in an unfamiliar setting and asked to function without glasses, I would not even be able to read a sign. It would quickly become obvious to everyone I was struggling, lost and afraid.

This same phenomenon that is true with natural eyes is true with spiritual eyes. If your spiritual vision is impaired, your ability to interact with and be fully engaged with your world is limited. As long as you remain in totally comfortable, well-known, familiar surroundings, you can probably fake it. People around you will not even be aware your vision is impaired. Your activity and motion may be convincing enough so others are unaware your destiny is limited by the inability to see beyond today. You may be so accustomed to living at this level of "low light/low revelation" you may not even realize your own restrictions. Day by day, you limit yourself to familiar paths, unwilling to venture beyond the borders of your comfort zone to discover the expanse of your purpose and move intentionally toward fulfilling your destiny.

When a circumstance occurs which suddenly places you in a foreign environment—a situation you have never encountered, a problem or crisis—your limitation is immediately felt. Instead of confidently navigating through the challenge, you find yourself groping around, paralyzed by fear and doubt, unsure of the next few steps in front of you. If your vision is unclear, your ability to complete your assignment is compromised.

FINDING CLARITY

When you realize you cannot see, when you grow weary of living with impaired vision, you must seek assistance from someone who can help you find the right prescription to bring things into focus. If you've ever been to an eye doctor, you know you sit behind his instrument while he asks you, "Does it look better with number one, or number two?"

"Number one," you say.

"Great," he replies. "How about this: number three or number four?"

He keeps offering you choices, allowing you to recognize how small distinctions in the shape of the lens can sharpen things and allow you to see clearly. Even small, incremental adjustments bring about a dramatic result.

Actually, you choose your own prescription. You determine what it takes to bring things into focus. Each time the doctor clicks through the options on his machine, he presents you with a choice—you get to state your preference. It is up to you to make the decision. The doctor examines you to be sure your eyes are healthy and disease free. Once the health is determined, he skillfully presents you with your options and guides you through the process until "Voila!" ... you can see!

I would like to play the role of optometrist for your spiritual eyes. By asking the right questions and pointing out small distinctions, I want to help you realize greater value in yourself. I want to help you enhance your ability to focus and bring clarity to the way you are designed. My hope is that together we will discover just the right prescription for your spiritual eyes and "Voila!" ... you will see!

DIALING IN TO PASSION, GIFTS, AND ASSIGNMENT

As believers, we are aware everything we do is connected to something greater than ourselves. We know our Creator has designed us. We have been taught we are fearfully and wonderfully made.[1] Before we were even formed in our mother's womb, God knew us.[2] We know God has plans for us—plans for good and not evil, to prosper us, to bring us a future and a hope.[3] We even know if we delight ourselves in the Lord, He will give us the desires of our heart![4]

There is much talk about purpose, destiny, and design. We understand we were born for something more than breathing, eating, sleeping, having children, and providing for them. We get it—there is greater purpose for our life—a calling or a destiny. God designed us for a purpose. Most of us are not clearly dialed in to what that greater purpose is.

God meant for passion, gifts, and purpose (or assignment) to work together. Purpose is not the reason we do something. Purpose is the specific thing we do—it is the *what*. It answers the question, "What am I here for?" It is the mission, the assignment—the works we are created to do! Down deep, we know we were created for a purpose.

Jesus told us the works He did, we would do also. Not only that, He told us we would do even greater works than He did.[5] When Jesus came to earth, He completed the works (the assignment) the Father gave Him to finish.[6]

This is where most of us get stuck. We have difficulty clearly defining our assignment, so we are unable to focus. Our vision is blurred. We cannot see the path to purpose, so we do our very best to walk in the general direction of loving God, worshipping God, and wanting to make a difference in the lives of others—setting people free. We likely have a vague sense of what we *ought* to do, but we stray away from what we *desire* to do, because it seems too carnal. So, we end up with a sense of guilt over how we manage our lives.

WHEN OUR VISION IS BLURRED, WE CANNOT SEE THE PATH TO PURPOSE.

This is backwards. It is like setting sail without a destination. Imagine leaving New York harbor bound for Europe, but sailing without knowledge of where in Europe you are to go. Without a specific port of call in mind, you would not know which heading to take beyond a general direction of "east." You could easily end up on the coast of Africa, far from Europe, and far from your supposed destination. All the while, you might feel you are making great progress, but you wind up missing the mark completely.

START AT PASSION

If purpose is the *what*, then passion is surely the *why*. We must begin at passion.

When people try to identify the destination (the *what*) first, there is an obligation to manufacture the passion to pursue it. This works against the way God designed and wired us.

How many people choose a course of study or career based on their parents' expectations or the possibility of achieving a certain level of income or prestige? For instance, say you have been told all your life you are going to grow up and be a doctor. You are told this so often you believe it. As a child seeking approval, you play doctor, and receive overwhelming positive feedback from your parents and others. When aunts and uncles and teachers ask you what you want to be when you grow up, you dutifully answer, "A doctor." A smile and an approving nod provides even more positive feedback.

What if in high school you discover you love the theater and public speaking? When you perform in front of people you come alive! When you give a speech or engage in a debate, your adrenalin rushes and you feel free. You can't get enough! But to get into the right college and then into medical school requires high performance in AP level science and mathematics. Involvement on the debate team and the drama club interferes with your ability to achieve at the top level of these classes.

You may be discouraged from pursuing your natural passion because it doesn't line up with the destiny prescribed for you by others' expectations. As a result, you drop out of these clubs and push down your desires, trying hard to get excited about your medical career. "I can help people," you tell yourself. "I can save lives." This is noble. It feels like the right thing to do. The sound track created in your head is used to psyche yourself up to pursue your chosen career.

Thirty years later, you are sitting in your office feeling frustrated and unfulfilled. You no longer have the energy to manifest a passion that wasn't in your DNA. You have spent your whole life pursuing a destiny that wasn't aligned with your original design. Now you are filled with regret. You push through your days, aware the price to pursue your dreams is too high to even think about.

Passion has nothing to do with fulfilling obligations or responsibilities. It isn't about making a paycheck or surviving. Passion is about the calling. Passion is the motivator behind the mission. Passion focuses us on "being" and not on "doing."

On the inside, you are wired for something. You were designed with innate desires. You are unique. You are one-of-a-kind. Your passion and desires are God-given. These are things which give you pure delight. Raw, unfiltered joy. Your passion moves you in ways others do not feel. Passion is your heart. It is the force which drives life through your body.

When a believer begins to function from their place of passion, something rises up on the inside to say, "Danger! You may be operating in the flesh. Is this really God?"

When you function inside of your passion, you will be challenged. You will be pressured to believe the proper way to pursue your destiny is to deny your desires. After all, isn't that what Jesus meant when He said, "If anyone desires to come after Me, let him deny himself, and take up his cross, follow Me"?[7]

The enemy of your soul wants you to believe your desires are evil and that pursuing those desires will take you off course. If he can convince you that your desires are self-serving and filled with temptation, he can convince you to abandon your passion. He can convince you that to be a good Christian you must reject your desires. His strategy goes like this: If you enjoy something too much, if it brings too much pleasure, it must not be of God. But that's not true! Enjoying the desires God has placed in your heart brings tremendous pleasure, both to you and to God.

The trouble comes when you confuse your values with your passion. Passion does not have a value system. Passion is neutral. Your values—your ethics, and the integrity with which you pursue your passion—allow for a sanctified manifestation of your purpose. When you confuse your values with your passion, you cannot get a clear picture of what you really want. You cannot understand what makes you fully alive if you are worried that your passion itself is evil.

Passion is pure. Passion is what drives people to achieve extraordinary things. No athlete ever won a gold medal without the passion to play their sport. They love it. They love it so much, they'll adjust everything else in their life—their diet, their social activities, their education—*everything* in order to pursue their dream.

All along your journey, you have experienced moments when you connect purely with this passion. There have been moments when you were 100% fully engaged, 100% fully alive. These were moments when you were quickened in your spirit and satisfied in your soul. Even if only for a moment, you connected to the heart of God and tasted your destiny. And having once tasted, it is now impossible to be satisfied to pursue any course that does not connect your passion, your gifts, and your purpose together.

In fact, the level of discomfort you are experiencing in your daily life is an indicator of how closely you are aligned with your destiny. Your family, friends, life events, circumstances, even your views of God may have shaped your path in a direction that is off course from God's intended design.

Do you feel trapped by patterns? Do responsibilities and situations squeeze you into circumstances beyond your control? If you feel like your path has been carved out for you and you are unsure whether or not this path leads to your destiny, let me encourage you. It is not too late. You can come into alignment with your destiny by making an intentional course correction. This starts by identifying your passion.

WHAT'S YOUR PASSION?

Make a list of the top five or ten things you really, *really* love to do, or would love to do if you had the time or money to pursue them. Now, **stop!** For this exercise, I don't want you to list things you think you *ought* to do, or even things that are spiritual—such as praying, reading the Word, or ministering to people. It isn't that you might not be passionate about these things, but for the believer, these are natural expressions of your love for God. For the moment I want you to concentrate on what really lights your fire. What makes you want to dance on the inside ... fist pump, high five, and celebrate?

What is it that gets your juices going? What activities do you engage in that make you feel completely authentic? What energizes you and leaves you feeling fully engaged and fully alive? What activity do you get involved in that makes you lose all track of time?

Remember, you are supposed to make a list of several things. Things you love.

Still struggling? Okay, here is some help.

- ◆ What are you so good at that other people notice and affirm you?

- ◆ What activities create positive feedback for you?

- ◆ What do people come to you for?

◆ What do they recognize as your "area"?
  Your "zone"? Your "expertise"?

These are clues to identify your passion! Take earning a paycheck out of the equation. For a moment, remove all the expectations of others. Give yourself permission to turn off all the voices inside your head (including your own) that have told you what you *should* do, what you *need* to do. Now, what would excite you enough to make you leap out of bed every morning just for the opportunity to re-engage with that activity?

This is your passion!

This gives you a key to **why** something is meaningful to you. What you are looking for is an environment … a job … an opportunity … whatever … something that will provide the resources you need so you have time to live doing the thing that makes you feel most alive. If you can get paid to do what you're passionate about, you'll never work another day in your life. You'll be doing what you love. You'll be engaged with things that bring you joy and fulfillment!

Purpose is the ultimate point of passion. Passion connects you to the heartbeat of God for your life and ties you into the purpose for which you were created. You must first be able to articulate your passion; THEN you can pursue how it fits in.

How do you get there?

NOSCE TE IPSUM
"KNOW THYSELF"

If purpose is the *what* and passion is the *why*, gifts, talents, and skills comprise the *how*.

Remember, we put purpose on the back burner. I wanted you to start by identifying your passion—what you absolutely love to do. I wanted you to discover your *why*. I encourage this because we were created to be human *beings* not human *doings*. If you get caught up in the "doing" part, before you are clear on the "being" part, you are not likely to taste the fullness of all God has for you.

You want to live fully engaged. You want to fulfill the purpose of God for your life. How do you do this?

Your gifts are a clue. These must work in harmony with your passion if you are to step into your destiny.

You were born wired for greatness. There is something unique about you. You have a "knack" for something. Perhaps it is a gift with words or a way with animals. Maybe you are good with your hands and can fix things, or technology comes easy for you. Maybe you can sing, dance, or play an instrument. Maybe you are good with numbers. You may excel at teaching, breaking difficult concepts down into simple steps. You might be sunny and optimistic where others see only gloom. There is some area where you have natural gifts and talents.

Your personality is singular. The way you look at life and interact with people is part of your wiring. Are you introverted or out-going, whimsical or calculated, reserved or energetic and willing to take risks? Are you commanding or inclusive? Are you direct or diplomatic? Impulsive or stable? No matter the answer, it is important information to know about yourself. Your personality is a key to unlocking your destiny. It is part of the design God etched into the overall blueprint of your life. It isn't an accident—God gave it to you intentionally.

Beyond natural gifts and personality, you also possess certain strengths. Whether you are an activator, achiever, developer, maximizer, learner, or relator, your mix of strengths blends together with your gifts and personality in a special chemistry—and the result is you!

This formula of natural gifts, natural strengths, and natural temperament is key to understanding God's distinctive plan for your life. The more you understand *how* you are wired, the easier it will be to tap into *why* you are wired this way, and *what* you can accomplish with this unique design. When you connect these together, you will engage with life at a much higher level.

Your skill set is a result of your experience and education. Skills are developed. Say you are not good with numbers, but your dad was an accountant and you were expected to carry on the family business. You devote your energy and education to becoming an accountant. You may develop the required skills to get the job done. You will not likely reach the level of mastery of someone who is pre-wired for numbers, has a love of details and passion for accuracy. Your job can become a grind instead of a joy.

Instead of being adept with numbers, perhaps you are naturally a good communicator, able to translate ideas into words others can understand and apply. How much better would it be to pour your energy into developing skills related to communication? How much fulfillment would you derive from a teaching or writing career instead of being an accountant?

If you focus on the things you love and are naturally bent toward, your efforts to develop these areas will yield mastery. If you can learn to cooperate with your natural wiring, you will excel. Not only that, but you will enjoy the journey along the way.

Passion should be directed at your gifts and developed skills. Passion will drive you to develop mastery in the areas where you are naturally gifted. Being able to function with mastery while doing something you love is one of the most rewarding things possible. Passion should push you to expand your skill set and progress toward expertise in the area where you were created to flourish. But passion must be present. If you completely engage your gifts and skills but fail to connect to your passion, you will fall short of fulfilling your destiny.

THE INTERSECTION OF PURPOSE

Take a look at your gifts (natural talents and developed skills) and intersect them with your passion (desires and dreams). You have likely discovered your path to purpose!

Your purpose, your assignment—that thing for which you were created—is your ultimate contribution to humanity. How do you connect with this?

"Aha!" Suddenly it becomes clear. If you can find a way to operate in the full measure of your passion and engage with the full abilities of your gifts and skills, you will be functioning in your destiny. You will be fully engaged. You will be fully alive. You will experience the force of God's favor and the blessings of obedience. You will walk in abundant life and be energized and mobilized to fulfill your calling.

Where these things intersect is where you will discover your assignment, your purpose. My friend, Lance Wallnau, describes this as *Level 10 Living*.[8] If you were to draw a vertical line to represent your developed skills and natural gifts, and then a horizontal line to represent your passion, you can see a clear path toward *Level 10 Living*—engaging the world with total fulfillment, clarity of assignment, and the greatest impact of influence. *(See Figure 1 on the following page.)*

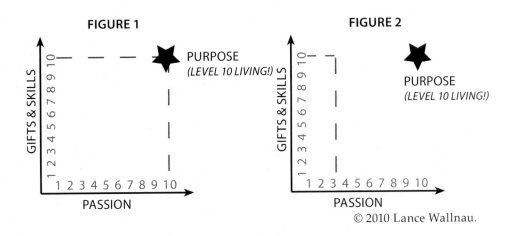

© 2010 Lance Wallnau.

You can see that if your work is engaging your gifts and skills at a level ten, but your passion is only engaged at a level three, you are not functioning in your purpose. Your full potential is not being accessed. *(See Figure 2 above.)* For true fulfillment, gifts and skills must intersect with passion at a high level.

This is why you must articulate your passion before you can have clarity concerning your purpose. You must also understand your gifts. You must know your strengths, and you must intentionally develop your skills. Where these intersect is where your greatest effectiveness lies.

There are a number of tools to help you do this.[9] You can access the Passion Process™, DiSC® Personality Profiles, The 5 Love Languages® Assessment, and StrengthsFinder 2.0®. There are profiles available covering everything from building confidence to managing stress, and from maximizing team roles to choosing a career aligned with your temperament. These can all assist with your personal growth and development. I cannot encourage you enough to invest yourself in the pursuit of clarity for your passion, your gifts, and your purpose.

You must intentionally participate in the design of your own future. You have the ability to rewrite your script—change the sound track inside your head—and step into your unlimited future. In the next chapter we will discuss intentional identity. You will learn how to celebrate your originality and the pure joy of adding your uniqueness to something greater than yourself.

Endnotes

1. Psalms 139:14.
2. Jeremiah 1:5.
3. Jeremiah 29:11.
4. Psalms 37:4.
5. John 14:12.
6. John 5:36.
7. Matthew 10:37-38 (NKJV).
8. *Level 10 Living* is available at www.lancelearning.com.
9. The Passion Process™ is available at www.lancelearning.com. The DiSC® Personality (and other related profiles) are available at: www.everythingdisc.com. The 5 Love Languages® Assessment is available at www.5lovelanguages.com/assessments/love. *StrengthsFinder 2.0* can be accessed at www.strengthsfinder.com.

CHAPTER TWO

INTENTIONAL IDENTITY

I celebrate the individuality of others. Pinpointing what makes someone special—their personality, their skills, their motivations, their perspective, even their history—gives me great joy. In fact, it is one of my passions. I have learned to develop this natural talent into a skill that serves me well as a personal branding consultant. I help people zero in on their passion, identify their strengths, their communication style, and their core message.

I have the privilege of helping others see what problems they are specifically gifted to solve, and then discover who has those problems. Together we create language to articulate this and find ways to monetize what they love so their employment can be rewarding and fulfilling. By dialing in to what makes someone stand out in a crowd, it is easy for me to build a brand around their "unique factor." It is quite often a matter of highlighting a combination of small distinctions that allows a person to be truly memorable and step into their calling with confidence.

The journey of discovery is exciting. As I work with clients and we unpack what makes them tick, ideas long dormant come bubbling to the surface. Dreams emerge; fear and frustration fade. Creativity and resourcefulness come bursting forth. New levels of energy are released as a result of becoming fully engaged. The possibility of living in alignment with their destiny—fully alive—begins to takes shape as a legitimate reality. It is exhilarating for me.

I love watching people begin to merge their passion and gifts in pursuit of their destiny. I get excited every time a person begins to see themselves as God sees them. When they come to understand what specialized architecture He used to fashion them, I feel like doing cartwheels and running laps. It is what makes me get up in the morning, ready to begin a new day.

It is important for you to know who you are in Christ and understand every promise and every blessing He has for you. I believe identity is precious, and thus should be stewarded as wisely and carefully as you steward money or time. You need to become intentional with your identity.

IDENTITY IS A GIFT

It is important for you to know all the elements God brought together in crafting your blueprint. You should take the time to learn all you can about your personality and how you interact with others. You should be aware of your communication style and how to bring weaknesses under control. Find out what your strengths are and how you can maximize them. Learn about your gift mix, your skill sets, even your love language. You should pay attention to your story: it is distinctive and creates a perspective only you possess. Your journey has equipped you with experiences and observations and lessons that are extremely valuable. You should know what you believe about God and why. You should explore your passions and articulate your dreams. If you view your identity as a gift from God, you will begin to treasure it. Your self-esteem, self-image, and even self-talk will begin to reflect the way God sees you and how you ought to see yourself.

You are rare and precious. You are one-of-a-kind. Your particular blend of experiences, skills, gifts, talents, anointing, and passion has an important role to play. You play the starring role in your life and only you can play it. There is no understudy for your part!

YOU PLAY THE STARRING ROLE IN YOUR LIFE AND ONLY YOU CAN PLAY IT. THERE IS NO UNDERSTUDY FOR YOUR PART!

Understanding your identity is the first step in becoming intentional with it. Once you have become aware of what makes you unique, the next step is to make sure you become congruent with that special blueprint. Once you have become acquainted with your authentic self—the self God intended you to be—the process of aligning your thoughts, your speech, and your actions to that pattern begins.

YOUR AUTHENTIC SELF

It is a journey, to be sure. We learn how to wear different masks appropriate for different situations. We are actually coached in this from the time we are children. As a child, I knew a certain behavior was expected from me at church, at Grandma's house, in a store, or when guests came over. If I didn't deliver on that expectation, unpleasant discipline was a certainty. This was right and proper, of course. Small children are always their authentic selves, and that self is unbridled, self-absorbed, and self-centered. It requires the guidance of loving parents to teach children how to yield selfish behavior to morally upright behavior.

The purpose of such discipline is not to learn how to "pretend" right behavior; it is to mold character and train a child to think of others. They must learn to see how their actions affect the world beyond them. However, though the intention is to develop character, children often learn to pretend to be a certain way in one setting, and a completely different way in another. Instead of truly developing character, a skill set is born—how to be the right thing to the right people at the right time. We learn to wear masks that hide and protect our true identity. We learn to act one way at work, another with friends, and a different way still at church or a PTA meeting. We learn which language and behavior is suitable for different situations or groups and how to wear the appropriate mask for a given time.

But wearing a mask takes energy—a lot of energy! The longer you wear one, or the more often you have to switch from one mask to another, the more tired and irritable you become. You only take the mask off in the comfort of your own home, around family or close friends—offering the worst version of yourself to the people you care about the most.

It doesn't have to be that way. The more intentional you become with your identity, the less the need to wear a mask exists. You can begin to function from a place of congruency—a place where your actions, attitudes, and motivations are aligned with the character of Christ, and your authentic self becomes appropriate in every setting. When your identity is congruent with God's design, there is never a need to wear a mask.

WHEN YOUR IDENTITY IS CONGRUENT WITH GOD'S DESIGN, THERE IS NEVER A NEED TO WEAR A MASK.

IDENTITY CRISIS

Not everyone follows through with the development of character, and in the absence of strong character, learning about how unique you are can have a negative effect. Celebrating your uniqueness is not an excuse for becoming

INTENTIONALITY—LIVE ON PURPOSE!

self-absorbed. Learning your strengths is not a reason to become proud or puffed up. Finding out about your personality type and communication style is not an excuse to force people into accepting you as you are without adjustment or awareness on your part. In fact, the more you understand about how and why God created you, the more your character should be refined, the closer your thoughts and actions should align to your authentic self. The more you learn about how you are wired to succeed, the more care you should take to eliminate all the things that are contrary and detrimental to God's perfect design. Humility should become your garment of choice. The pursuit of wisdom should take a high priority.

> CELEBRATING YOUR UNIQUENESS IS NOT AN EXCUSE FOR BECOMING SELF-ABSORBED.

Most people I encounter suffer from seeing themselves as "less than," therefore not stepping into their assignment effectively. Others see themselves as "greater than," therefore assessing so much value to their assignment, their strengths, and their style that they devalue the uniqueness and purpose of everyone else around them.

As much as I love to help people articulate their uniqueness and become excited about their individuality, the down side for me is that some suddenly seem to take up all the available oxygen in a room. Once they have gone through the process to identify what makes them special, they want to leverage this to expand their influence or promote themselves, walking on the mission and mantle of others. Essentially, they build up their own kingdom, not God's. Instead of stepping into their destiny and learning how their distinctively shaped piece fits into the larger puzzle crafted by God, they pervert their destiny, twisting their passion and gifts into something self-serving.

An undesirable identity crisis is created when someone discovers all they have to offer, but is unwilling to yield to the greater purpose of their uniqueness and surrender it to something larger than themselves.

CHRIST IS PREEMINENT

Above all, Christ must have preeminence in your life. When you are truly aware that you are a creation and not the Creator, it is impossible not to bow in reverent humility. You are not your own. You have been bought with a price.[1] When you recognize this, it is impossible to view your life and your identity as anything but a stewardship. You belong to God. Everything about you is by His design, crafted for His enjoyment and His purpose. The sooner you can learn what that is and begin to cooperate with it, the more joy you will experience.

Being intentional with your identity means you recognize you are a piece, not the whole. When you realize your extraordinary blend belongs to One who is greater, you understand that submitting your identity to something larger and greater than yourself is completely safe. There is no danger you will lose your identity by submitting it to the Master's design. In fact, it is quite the opposite.

Consider a mosaic. Each tile or piece of glass is beautiful all by itself. It has a specific shape, particular coloring, and interesting patterns. You could easily admire each individual piece, recognizing its singular value and worth.

When a piece of the mosaic surrenders itself to the artist, it submits to his craftsmanship, trusting placement in exactly the right spot. We are His workmanship, prepared by God.[2] Adjacent to other pieces, we will be perfectly suited and fitly joined to create a grand design. We become so much greater as part of a whole than we could ever be as individual pieces.

By yielding your perfectly rare, beautiful, individual identity to something larger than yourself, you get to be celebrated and enjoyed in a way that would never have been possible had you remained alone.

INTENTIONAL SUBMISSION

I am fascinated by beautiful architecture. Visiting the great cathedrals of Europe is high on my bucket list. I have lovingly studied pictures and read about their architecture and history. I genuinely appreciate the level of craftsmanship involved and the dedication and sacrifice of whole towns to erect these beautiful structures in order to glorify God.

Most of these were not built by a single generation of craftsmen. It isn't like today where you visit a city and return a year later to find a giant building standing where there was once nothing but a vacant lot.

When the cathedrals were built, it took thousands of workers decades (or even centuries) to erect. Construction of Cologne Cathedral commenced in 1248 but was halted in 1473, leaving it unfinished. Work recommenced in the 19th century and it was finally completed to the original plan in 1880—632 years after construction began.[3] Workers were too numerous to count and their names do not appear on any plaques or commemorative monuments. Many of them worked their whole lives on a project they would never have the privilege of seeing finished. They made huge sacrifices without receiving any credit for their work. Their passion was fueled by a desire to please God. They had faith that He saw and valued everything they did for His glory. And yet, their work remains, enduring the tests of time and war and politics. The structures still stand, pointing their beautiful spires upward to God.

While studying the great cathedrals of Europe, I read an intriguing story, and though I have researched, I cannot find the source or I would gladly give credit. The story told of a wealthy man who was visiting a cathedral during its construction. The rich man noticed one of the workers painstakingly carving an exquisite bird on the inside of one of the beams. The wealthy man, a patron who had contributed heavily to the project, scolded the worker, "Why are you spending so much time carving something so intricate on a beam that is going to be completely covered by the roof? No one is ever even going to see it!"

The story goes that the workman finished carving the section of wing he was working on before turning his gaze on the rich man. With softness in his eyes and a catch in his throat he replied, "Because God sees." He then turned his full attention back to the tiny bird he was carving.

How many of us would be willing to contribute the best of our skills without any recognition to the greatness of something no one would ever see? How many of us are willing to submit our passion and our gifts to a purpose so much greater than ourselves that we completely trust God's plan and give everything we have for the pure joy of giving it?

When our greatest affirmation comes from within, and we are completely secure in our identity, our usefulness to God multiplies. We can easily align with His purpose because we completely trust that His purpose is also His best for us. There is no need to manipulate people or circumstances to achieve status or title or recognition. There is no need to fear going unnoticed or unappreciated. There is no chafing if promotion doesn't come as quickly as we would like or think we deserve. Serving God for the joy of pleasing Him becomes its own reward.

Intentional identity, to me, is about understanding the value of who God has created you to be, and being aware of everything unique and special that went into your exact design. Then, once you understand and become totally comfortable celebrating who you are in Him, you submit the whole package back to Him. You are content to allow Him to perfectly place you in His mosaic exactly where He wants to ... or even to assign you to carving a tiny bird on a beam that only He will see and enjoy.

Whatever your assignment, however great or small, seen or unseen, know that in God's eyes your identity is precious. Your assignment—your purpose and destiny—is His intentional expression of love toward you.

It isn't your visibility, but your contribution that matters. Some of the most influential people I know don't have an official "following." They have never written a book, cured a disease, or won a gold medal, but they live their lives filled with purpose. They do what they do best and make a difference wherever they go.

Endnotes

1. 1 Corinthians 6:19-10.

2. Ephesians 2:10.

3. Retrieved from: http://www.sacred-destinations.com/germany/cologne-cathedral.

INTENTIONAL IDENTITY IS UNDERSTANDING
THE VALUE OF WHO GOD CREATED
YOU TO BE, AND BEING AWARE OF
EVERYTHING UNIQUE AND SPECIAL THAT
WENT INTO YOUR EXACT DESIGN.

CHAPTER THREE

INTENTIONAL CHOICES

"It will cost something to walk slowly in the parade of the ages while excited men of time rush about confusing motion with progress. But it will pay in the long run."

—A.W. Tozer

Every decision you make directs your time, energy, influence, and resources toward something and away from something else.

You are probably careful about the big choices. When confronted with an obvious life-altering fork in the road, you likely pause to weigh your options. You are aware that the choice you make will have long-lasting impact on the quality of your life. When it is time to consider getting married, taking a new job, or making a major move or some other important life change, you do not address that decision casually. You collect the facts. You seek counsel (or at least opinions) from friends or mentors. You pray about it and ask others to pray about it with you. You want to do the right thing. You measure how the decision will affect you and those close to you. You understand that a major decision has major repercussions on your life. You inherently know that down the road you will be able to point back to this decision and see measurable rewards or consequences for having made the choice.

We can all look back and identify major choices that directed our lives—both choices we made for ourselves and choices significant others made for us. Most of these major decisions were made consciously. Right or wrong, good or bad, choices were made.

THE PERIL OF "NON" CHOICES

Not making a choice is the same thing as making a choice. Not making a choice is simply deflecting the responsibility for the choice onto someone else. It is choosing to allow someone or something else to choose for you. For example:

◆ Ignoring a bill is choosing not to pay it.

◆ Allowing someone to cross your boundaries and control your time is choosing to surrender your time to someone else's priorities.

◆ Not preparing for foul weather is choosing to walk around wet …

… you get the point.

There are consequences for "non-choices." They set off an unstoppable chain reaction of cause and effect. Yet, instead of owning the consequences, you feel justified in deflecting the responsibility onto the person or circumstance that was the cause for your particularly unpleasant effect.

◆ You were charged a late fee by the "blood-sucking, price-gouging" utility company. This resulted in an overdraft when your mortgage payment cleared the scheduled automatic withdrawal, creating embarrassment, more late fees, and bank charges. Stupid electric company!

◆ You were running late to your dental appointment because the Booster Club left a message reminding you to bring brownies for the football team's bake sale, "… and remember—our bake sale is an honored tradition. Store-bought baked goods are not allowed. Thank you for your support!" You rush around to get ready for your appointment and burn the brownies while you are getting dressed. Frustrated, you cut through a parking lot to avoid a traffic light and make up for lost time. Sadly, an officer notices this and stops you, issuing a ticket for the violation. This takes so long you miss your appointment. You now have burned brownies that no one can sell, a toothache, and a traffic ticket. Stupid Booster Club!

◆ You wore your best suit to the interview. You are excited. You've been looking forward to this! You notice the grey clouds, but have no idea where the umbrella is and don't want to be late. You pull into the parking lot just as it begins to rain. There are no spots available near the door and you have to park far away. Even though you sprint like a track star, you get soaking wet. You walk into the office panting, your hair dripping onto your collar, and your mood is now as stormy as the rain clouds outside. It doesn't go well. Stupid rain!

In truth, all these "non-choices" were choices. Had you opened the bill and paid it, there would have been no negative consequences. The check wouldn't have bounced and there would never have been a late fee.

Had you said to the Booster Club, "No, I'm afraid I won't be able to help you out this time," you would have been on time to the dentist, gotten your toothache fixed, and avoided the traffic ticket.

Had you put an umbrella in the car (or stored an umbrella in the car in the first place) you could have avoided that entire scenario. Your opportunity to make the right first impression at the interview would not have been sabotaged by circumstances you felt were beyond your control.

There is no such thing as not choosing. Not choosing is a choice.

THE TROUBLE WITH CASUAL CHOICES

You make hundreds of choices every day: what to eat, what to wear, what to watch, what to say, what to listen to, where to go, when to sleep, what calls to accept, etc.

Most of our choices are made with very little thought. There isn't time (or energy) to weigh out all the options, or consider how a minor choice will affect you for the rest of the day, let alone the rest of your life. You make these choices instinctively or on a whim based on your mood, or the mood of others. They are small choices. In the grand scheme of things they don't matter ... or do they?

- It is 3:00 in the afternoon and you haven't eaten since breakfast. You are hungry. You spy donuts in the break room and before you realize it, you have downed three of them.

- "Sure, I would love to do lunch!" You accept the date on your calendar without even thinking about it. "That will be fun!"

- It's *Shark Week* on the Discovery Channel! It's educational; you love sharks! You stay up late watching these amazing creatures. You just can't get enough!

Harmless. Right?

Maybe. It is true that such casual decisions will probably not shatter the cosmic time line. But a string of casual decisions can take you off course inch by careless inch until the flow of your time, energy, and resources is directed in a completely different direction from where you want to go. When a satellite dish on earth is misdirected by just one degree, it will miss the signal being sent from space by more than 800 miles. Look at the illustration below.

FIGURE 1

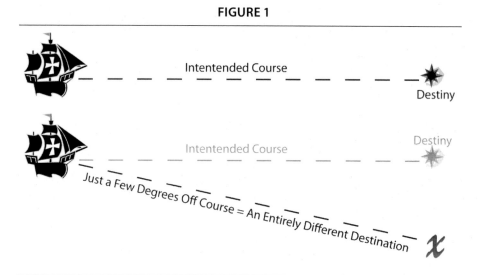

To binge on donuts one afternoon will not result in Type II Diabetes. But eating whatever presents itself when you are in the crisis moment of hunger will create a habit of poor nutrition, high caloric intake, and oral gratification. In time you will find yourself overweight, sluggish, and subject to physical ailments. If you allow the moment to dictate your casual choice, you will become a slave to what feels or tastes good right now instead of determining the stewardship of your own body.

Lunch dates are great! Time with friends and family is wonderful and we should make time for relationships. There must be room for spontaneity in your life. However, some people live so serendipitously they sabotage their destiny one six-dollar sandwich and five-dollar cup of coffee at a time. Because there is no intentional vision toward a long-term goal (such as home ownership, an exotic vacation, a retirement plan, or whatever), eating out regularly at modest establishments seems totally harmless. I know many people who remain poor, one movie, one video game, one latté, and one designer clothing item at a time. Their purchases are casual—on a whim, to make them feel better about themselves—or "just because." There is nothing intentional about their purchasing decisions.

Consider this. Perhaps budget isn't an issue keeping you from accomplishing your purpose. Maybe you have a burning desire to invent something, solve an important problem, or write a book. You keep telling yourself you want time to exercise, take a class, or spend more time with your family. If you accept every invitation to lunch or dinner, attend every conference, show up for every birthday, say yes to every available opportunity to minister or socialize, you will never have time for what is important. You will repeatedly put things off and excuse yourself with, "I just don't have the time." Even when everything you say yes to happens to be good, the sum total of your choices can keep you on the edge of stress and feeling out of control rather than living a rich, full, purposeful life.

Casual decisions as minor as staying up too late to watch one more episode of your favorite program can indicate a pattern of neglecting what is important to satisfy what is present. There is nothing wrong with watching television or movies. I love them! In fact, I get some of my best ideas while watching the creative work of others. But there comes a time to turn them off. There are seasons when you must restrict the volume of entertainment you enjoy—mindless, unproductive hours. Remaining "plugged in" to cell phones, social media, the 24-hour news cycle, and other distractions will pull you off course, even if only by a few degrees. If you are clear about your destiny and resolved to your purpose, casual decisions that impact your mission are a luxury you cannot afford.

> IF YOU ARE CLEAR ABOUT YOUR DESTINY AND RESOLVED TO YOUR PURPOSE, CASUAL DECISIONS THAT IMPACT YOUR MISSION ARE A LUXURY YOU CANNOT AFFORD.

When you become clear about your purpose and can identify your strengths, temperament, gifting and passion, you will begin to make choices with intentionality.

THE BEAUTY OF INTENTIONAL CHOICES

Intentional choices keep you on track. They help you stay the course so you can reach your destiny and still enjoy the journey along the way. Right now you might be thinking that it sounds like too much work. Do I really mean for you to carefully weigh out every single decision you make throughout the day?

Actually, it is easier than you think. If you are saving to buy a house or car, it is easy to say no to five-dollar coffee. You can take a thermos of the good stuff with you and still enjoy the experience.

If you want to lose weight, planning your food in advance is a good strategy. That way you are prepared when hunger strikes and you won't sabotage your big goals for the expediency of the moment.

It is much easier to say no to the casual lunch date or request to be a volunteer if you have a significant project you want to accomplish. You will have already set aside the time you need to develop the project. You will only say yes to what doesn't interfere. You can absolutely leave room for social interaction and community involvement, but when you establish your boundaries, you release yourself from guilt when someone tries to cross them and you must say, "No."

When I coach people on developing their intellectual property (finding a way to monetize their passion and gifts), the first thing I have them do is to set appointments with themselves on their own calendar. I ask them to find time each week to block off in order to develop their project—content, book, teaching, program, or whatever. I have them treat this as a hard appointment that cannot be moved or interrupted. I know if they will assign this time as a priority and communicate to others they are unavailable during this time, they will get the job done! People who have put off a dream for years find they make huge strides toward their goals in just a few months. Why? They become intentional with their choices. They stop allowing casual opportunities to take them off course and sabotage their dream. You can too!

In the next chapter we are going to discuss the power of intentional neglect and the importance of being clear about what you want—both now and later. You will find that if you are dialed into your goals with clear vision, it takes the work out of making the right choices.

INTENTIONAL NEGLECT

"Procrastination is the assassination of motivation." I have no idea who said this first, but whenever I catch myself putting something off, this quote pops into my consciousness and spurs me to take action. I find I procrastinate for one of two reasons: 1) the task is overwhelming, or 2) the task is unpleasant.

Putting something off feels good only for the moment. When you neglect to do what needs to be done, you can easily lose your awareness of its importance. In fact, procrastination is like a vacuum that sucks the energy out of intentionality. Problems ignored escalate until they become crises—requiring more time, energy, and resources to solve than if they had been addressed at the proper time. Opportunities pass by because you were unprepared to act—leaving you wondering why other people seem to get all the breaks. Letters you should have written, contacts you should have made, people with whom you should have networked slide to the back burner, because you neglected them—unintentionally.

Life happens fast. Energy is directed to things urgent and misdirected by distractions, pleasant or unpleasant. Without being consciously aware, you can find yourself in a downward spiral of lowered productivity, careless inefficiency, missed deadlines, stress, and a frustrated sense of personal failure. When you are a slave to your own schedule, your dreams grow elusive and destiny takes a detour.

WHEN YOU ARE A SLAVE TO YOUR OWN SCHEDULE, YOUR DREAMS GROW ELUSIVE AND DESTINY TAKES A DETOUR.

Neglecting the important things in your work life is like a virus. It spreads into neglect of things in your family life and your faith life. Even your own personal health and wellness can be affected. The things you would truly *like* to do get trumped by the things you *have* to do. You find yourself living behind the eight ball, never quite satisfied with your days. It is a vicious cycle, and without an intentional redirection, it is an unending cycle.

"I don't have time!" is the unrecognized confession that your priorities are confused. Your careless investment of moments becomes a mountain of wasted time. Your life spins out of control. You find yourself constantly playing catch-up. The stress load becomes unbearable.

Too often people look outside themselves, wanting a dramatic change for an unfulfilling life. Blame is assessed. Maybe a divorce results, a major job change is made, or a mid-life crisis develops. No matter how dramatic the change, if priorities are still neglected, important responsibilities will go unachieved and success will not come.

Time is neither friend nor foe. Either you use what you have well, or you waste it. You have only 24 hours each day to live your life, enjoy your family, accomplish your goals, and rest your body. Each of us has 168 hours a week—no more, no less. You cannot manufacture time. You cannot be awarded extra minutes for good behavior. Neither can you be assessed penalty minutes for bad decisions. At the stroke of midnight, tomorrow becomes today, and whatever you failed to accomplish of your agenda is transferred to the future.

How do you keep from being caught in the cycle of procrastination? I find that one of the best tools to accomplish this is neglect—intentional neglect.

"Wait a minute!" I can hear you say. "Didn't you just warn me about the evils of procrastination? What's the difference between procrastination and neglect?"

Actually, there is a h-u-g-e difference between *procrastination* and *intentional neglect*. Procrastination is careless neglect, overlooking the obvious and important in favor of the expediency of the moment. Intentional neglect is the ability to look at everything that must be accomplished, prioritize those things effectively, and eliminate the ones that do not fulfill your purpose, accomplish your goals, and bring you a successful outcome.

I want to share six specific strategies that have worked for me. These are tested principles you can employ to overcome procrastination or careless neglect. Trust me when I tell you, I am preaching to myself. Intentionality is not a once and done deal. It is a constant companion of the successful and a consistent supervisor of those who achieve their destiny.

Few, if any, get to the pinnacle of their dreams by accident. Success takes effort. Opportunity meets preparation. If you prepare as though opportunities were already manifest, when they come your way you can step into them and capture all the available momentum. They will not take you by surprise. You will have an eye on the horizon and be well stocked to launch your journey at a moment's notice. If you wait for an opportunity to appear before you prepare, when it comes, you will find yourself behind the curve, struggling to catch up and likely falling behind and missing it altogether.

1. ACKNOWLEDGE YOU CAN'T DO IT ALL

The idea that you will eventually get caught up with everything is a myth. It's impossible! I spent years with more work facing me than I could reasonably expect to accomplish within a practical amount of time. I tried to compensate by working longer and later. I pushed myself harder, juggled my family, and sacrificed my health. I was so unwilling to let anyone down (including myself) that I set an impossible pace. I neglected my own calling and damaged the important resources God had given me. By trying to do it all, I compromised my rest. Without sufficient rest or "down time," my creativity, ingenuity, resourcefulness, and concentration were all diminished. Time I did spend with my family was overshadowed by guilt for all the time I was away from them. I lived in frustration and was constantly under stress. For every item I completed, five more were added. No matter how hard I worked, I could never catch up ... and the idea of being ahead was a joke!

If this story strikes a chord in you, it may be time to have a heart-to-heart talk with yourself. Your workload is never static. It continues to grow and change. You finish one task, and before it's done, another takes its place. Your "To Do" list is constantly filling up with fresh new tasks, new challenges, and new responsibilities.

We fill our calendars with work, family, social, and community responsibilities. I constantly run into people who fully schedule every day and night. They are often double-booked and race from place to place. Never fully present anywhere they go, they keep one eye on their watch, calculating just when they have to leave to be on time for the next thing. There are no margins. There is no time to rest or regenerate. There is no time to enjoy the moment as they rush to meet the next obligation.

Recognizing your limitations forces you to become deliberate in choosing your tasks and accepting commitments. This is especially true if you are a self-employed entrepreneur.

RECOGNIZING YOUR LIMITATIONS FORCES YOU TO BECOME DELIBERATE IN CHOOSING YOUR TASKS AND ACCEPTING COMMITMENTS.

Constant financial demands challenge you to accept every client, every job—whether it is a right fit for you or not. In the hopes of growing your business to a level where you can expand and find some freedom, it is easy to con yourself into taking on a load too great to handle.

Those who work within a company or organization can face a similar problem. The demand for elevated productivity places a significant load on a work-force. Overtime re-muneration is far less expensive to a company than hiring, training, paying, and providing benefits for extra personnel. Because people have overextended their finances, they take on extra hours—double-time pay is very inviting. But while you work overtime to pay the bills, the clock continues ticking on other things of significant importance. Things like family, faith, and fulfillment. The things that stir your passion and make you feel fully alive get lost in the pursuit of doing more than can reasonably be accomplished. Stop trying to do it all.

2. ACCEPT THE FACT THAT SOME THINGS WON'T GET DONE

You will have to make peace with the fact that you must leave some things undone. This strategy lies at the heart of self-preservation. For the sake of your own sanity, you must accept the fact that you are not Superman. ♫ ♪ Dot-da-da-DA! ♪ ♫

This is a difficult strategy to embrace because some of the things, in fact, most of the things you want to do, are good things. Some of them are very good things. Consider that some of these things may just not be your things, or perhaps they are not "now" things. How do they relate to your big picture? Do they move you toward your destiny or away from it?

Good things must sometimes be sidelined in favor of better things, and better things may need to be passed on in favor of the best things. You cannot do everything if you are going to succeed in fulfilling your destiny. Having your own matrix of purpose is a strategic tool to help you evaluate which tasks you should do and which you must pass on to achieve your purpose.

3. PRACTICE WORKLOAD TRIAGE

On the battlefield, medics have to decide where to apply their limited resources. In emergency medical situations, doctors and nurses do as well. When caring for a single patient, a doctor can freely focus all efforts on that individual. But when a bus crashes and 12 ambulances roll in, such undivided care is not possible. They can't help everyone at the same time, and the most important cases must go first. This is called triage.

Triage is simply determining who can survive with little or no medical care, who must have immediate medical care to survive, and who is going to perish no matter how much care they are given. Performing triage forces medical personal to ignore two groups and focus on only those who require immediate medical care to survive.

This is an important strategy to follow when your work-load spills "over the top." It is the essence of intentional neglect. In spite of all you can do to address your world with intentionality, there are times when things pile up and spin out of control. At those times, it is important for you to know which things you can safely put on hold, which things you should completely ignore, and which things demand your immediate attention and intervention. This is workload triage.

QUICK AND ACCURATE EVALUATION OF YOUR SITUATION ALLOWS YOU TO FOCUS YOUR BEST ENERGIES ON THOSE THINGS WHICH CANNOT BE IGNORED.

Quick and accurate evaluation of your situation allows you to focus your best energies on those things which cannot be ignored. It also gives you the responsibility of communicating with those who got left "on hold." They, too, are your responsibility, and when the moment quiets, you will be able to return to meet those needs. At some point (not in the midst of the overload), you will be required to communicate with clients, supervisors, family, or committees. When you do, you will have more than an excuse. You will be able to present a reason why they were put at the end of the line. Most people respond with understanding when given the consideration of honest communication.

4. KEEP PRIORITIES STRAIGHT

When I was a teenager, my parents required me to read Stephen Covey's *7 Habits of Highly Successful People*. This book made a lasting impression on me, particularly the section dealing with the "tyranny of the urgent." I learned that if I allowed the things that were loudest (most urgent) to control my time, I would never be able to address the things that were most important to me. Mr. Covey had four categories: a) Urgent and Important, b) Important but Not Urgent, c) Urgent but Not Important, and d) Not Urgent and Not Important.

I have learned to schedule my day beginning with "Urgent and Important." Next I focus on tasks that are "Important but Not Urgent." If there is any room left, then I can move on to "Urgent but Not Important," and I am learning to ignore the "Not Urgent and Not Important" altogether. I consider tasks in light of my goals and priorities. If I allow what is urgent or important to other people to circumvent what I know is urgent or important to me, I become a slave to their priorities and neglect my own. I am empowered by making my own choices.

5. PRACTICE INTENTIONAL NEGLECT

This is the heartbeat of this chapter. All too often, people practice the opposite—unintentional neglect or procrastination. They overlook, bypass, or forget to become engaged with specific responsibilities. They find themselves consistently being late in meeting their deadlines or meeting them under undue stress at a high cost of energy or resources.

No one really likes this behavior, particularly those who are counting on you to accomplish a task. But this inevitably happens when you fail to practice intentional neglect. You must decide **in advance** you will not focus on the wrong tasks.

"But," you may ask, "what about tasks I don't think are important when someone else does?" That is a great question! Every time you are approached with a task (a contract or proposal, a circumstance, or an opportunity), it will most assuredly be important to someone. Specifically, it is either important or urgent (or both) to the person who approaches you. Consider it in light of your big picture. Respect your destiny enough to say no to things that do not fit your course.

Sometimes people press unimportant things onto your shoulders just to remove the responsibility from their own. If you accept those, you become a hapless victim. You must become intentional in neglecting, disregarding, or avoiding responsibilities that do not fall within your priorities. This is critical for the preservation of your available time. Every time you allow someone else's priorities to be super-imposed over your own, you will be frustrated as you are pushed further and further off course—away from your passion and your purpose. Overwhelmed by others' expectations and priorities, you will wake up one day and think, "How did I get here? How did this happen?"

An intentional "NO!" is one of the most strategic decisions you can make to achieve success. This is extremely hard for some people to do. When you overextend yourself, at some point you will fail. If you find yourself feeling guilty when you say no, or regretfully saying yes when you would like to say no, it is time to reframe your priorities.

6. STAY ON TASK

We live in a multi-tasking world. Truthfully, you cannot actually do more than one thing at a time, even though you may have two or more things going at the same time. You may be answering an email while on the telephone with someone else and a file is uploading in the background. Divided attention is just that—divided. Have you ever sent a text or email to the wrong person? Transferred money from or to the wrong account? Run a red light while talking on your mobile phone? Your attention will always be on what you are doing presently. Diverting your attention to something else can create all sorts of problems.

Technology has made it possible for us to have several things going on at once. Still, you must integrate thoughts into a single stream of conscious effort in order to be effective. Try focusing on four targets at a time with one arrow and see how good your aim is.

I love watching the television show *M*A*S*H*. In one episode, Charles Emerson Winchester was pontificating about his medical prowess—which was unquestionable. Someone complained that he didn't move fast enough. With complete unapologetic confidence he replied, "I do one thing at a time. I do it very well, and then I move on." True greatness!

Clarity is the first step. You need to have clarity regarding your purpose. Understanding your passion and connecting that to your purpose is the basis for establishing your priorities. Write them down. Communicate them with your spouse, your children, and anyone else who is a significant part of your life. You must know what is truly important to you, and then you must be willing to focus your life if you are going to achieve your destiny.

UNDERSTANDING YOUR PASSION AND CONNECTING THAT TO YOUR PURPOSE IS THE BASIS FOR ESTABLISHING YOUR PRIORITIES.

Learning the art of intentional neglect will liberate you from trying to be all things to all people. It will create margins in your life for rest and regeneration, and give you room to respond to unexpected opportunities.

It will allow you to focus on what is important—free from guilt for eliminating things that do not matter. Your productivity will increase. Your creativity will thrive. Your effectiveness will be elevated and your influence will expand. Learn to intentionally neglect the unimportant and you will enjoy the results of having both the time and the energy to do what you desire.

In the next chapter we will cover intentional relationships. Your relationships are also a product of your choices. You have the power to choose concerning every person present in your life. Cultivating intentional relationships will pay rich dividends.

INTENTIONAL NEGLECT WILL ALLOW YOU
TO FOCUS ON WHAT IS IMPORTANT—
FREE FROM GUILT FOR ELIMINATING
THINGS THAT DO NOT MATTER.

INTENTIONAL RELATIONSHIPS

Greater love has no man than this, than to
lay down one's life for his friends.
John 15:13 NKJV

Relationships bless our lives immeasurably. Just try to imagine your life totally isolated and living apart from people. What a desolate, meaningless existence that would be!

After creating Adam, God said, *"It is not good that man should be alone; I will make him a helper comparable to him."*[1] From the beginning, relationships were part of God's intentional design for humankind. We were not created to live alone. Family was established in the Garden—one flesh union producing offspring is part of the original plan.[2]

We have relationships with people on many levels, from casual acquaintances to life-long, intimate alliances. Some people in our lives God clearly brought our way. These people enrich and enhance us with abundant measure. Others seem to casually find their way into our circle and we aren't quite sure how or why they got there. Others still seem mission critical to the enemy to sabotage our joy and hinder our success—as though they were sent to buffet us and make us miserable.

The benefits of becoming intentional with your relationships are overwhelming. I have heard it said that family are people you are stuck with and friends are the family you choose. Regardless of your definition for friends or family, you have choices concerning your relationships. So choose. Make good choices. Make intentional choices.

HEALTHY BOUNDARIES

Robert Frost said, "Good fences make good neighbors." For relationships to flourish and be mutually beneficial, clear boundaries are the key.

A healthy boundary establishes an open space where you begin and the other person ends. It allows you to exercise personal freedom. It keeps you safe from manipulation, control, and abuse. Setting boundaries requires clearly communicating expectations and limits. Signs of a healthy relationship are respecting differences, focusing on the best qualities and interests of both parties, maintaining balance, having freedom to spend time with other people, open communication, and the ability to adapt to changes in the relationship. If you find yourself relying too heavily on a partner or friend for happiness, experiencing jealousy or possessiveness, placing blame, focusing on the worst qualities of each other, unable to express your needs, or unable to give (or receive) affirmation, then it is time to step back and establish clear boundaries.

You cannot force healthy behavior on others, so you must remain aware and alert to make sure your relationships are healthy and strong. You must be careful to choose friends who edify you and believe in your dreams. Surrounding yourself with people who pull you down or hold you back is like having a weight around your neck. Spending significant amounts of time with people who are negative or have damaging habits will limit your success.[3] Like begets like. You tend to become like the people you spend the most time with.

Respect your destiny enough to be intentional with your relationships. It may be necessary to pull back from or eliminate relationships that hinder you from stepping into your calling or completing your assignment. Evaluate your relationships and determine if some necessary endings are required.

RESPECT YOUR DESTINY ENOUGH TO BE INTENTIONAL WITH YOUR RELATIONSHIPS.

MENTORS

*"Tell me and I forget, teach me and I may
remember, but involve me and I learn."*

Benjamin Franklin

Mentors are a gift. Whether the relationship is formed naturally or formally, having someone take an active interest in your growth and development is priceless.

The progression of your life will require many mentors. Some mentors may be in your life for a short season with a specific focus, while others may be with you for the long haul. A mentor committed to your success will constantly challenge you to improve and expand how you think. They will awaken your mind to new possibilities and encourage you to dream. They will teach you skills and create opportunities for you to develop them. They will demonstrate an interest in your success and be committed to your highest good.

Seek out mentors. It is rare (and precious) for someone to just fall into your life and take on a significant mentoring role. Find someone who is already successful in an area where you want to grow and get close to them. Pursue them. Ask them to mentor you. Learn from them. Honor their gift. Honor their experience and their wisdom. If they find you are eager to learn and willing to listen, chances are they will cheerfully pour into you.

I consider Winston Churchill a mentor, though we never met. He lived before my time. Even if we had been contemporaries, my chances of meeting him would have been slim, but I am inspired by his life. I studied him—his work and his writing. By honoring his contribution and intentionally internalizing his wisdom and perspective, I chose to make him a mentor. Because feedback is not possible, this isn't the highest form of mentoring, but it demonstrates an important point. You can seek out the expertise of others— living or dead—through books, seminars, and training. When you are intentional about your development, you actively place yourself into the role of mentee. If you find yourself without access to a flesh-and-blood mentor willing to invest themselves into your life, do not let this hinder you. The books you read, the messages you hear (and apply) will mold you in much the same way a mentor relationship can.

Mentor others. Just as you should always make sure you have people pouring into your life, you should also be pouring yourself into the lives of others. Duplicate yourself in someone else. Mentoring others will push you. You never learn a subject quite so well as when you must prepare to teach it to someone else. Mentoring others will keep the tip of your arrow sharp. It will force you to pay attention to the fact that other people are paying attention to you!

Mentoring is serving. Jesus said, "For even the Son of Man came not to be served, but to serve others and to give

His life as a ransom for many."[4] Jesus touched the world, but He mentored His disciples. He had a small group of men He poured into with intentional purpose. We should do the same.

INVEST YOURSELF

Invest yourself into friends and family. Connect with people at every opportunity. Let others know how important they are to you. Give yourself away. It is impossible to empty yourself of love. The more you give, the more it fills you up.

Neglect or indifference can cause significant drift in important friendships. Relationships have the power to transform our lives and make them infinitely more productive and meaningful. Intentional investment of time and focus is required to keep relationships strong.

The quality of your relationships can be directly related to your level of personal awareness and the awareness of others. The next chapter will challenge you to practice intentional awareness.

Endnotes

1. Genesis 2:18.
2. Genesis 2:23-24.
3. 1 Corinthians 15:33.
4. Mark 10:45.

CHAPTER SIX

INTENTIONAL AWARENESS

Once you start practicing present-moment awareness, you will notice miracles large and small happening all around you. The more you notice, and the more aware you become, the more depth your life takes on. The deeper your life is anchored in awareness and observation, the more in tune your heart will be with the events taking place around you. You will operate at a level of harmony, synchrony, rhythm, and pace.

Dr. Mark Chironna

There is a voice inside your head—a sound track of self-talk playing continuously. You may not even recognize it is playing, but it is there. Thoughts wash through your mind at an astounding pace. Negative thoughts drain your energy and keep you from being present in the moment. They sabotage your confidence and limit your willingness to take risks or venture into unknown territory. The more you give in to negative thoughts, the more powerful they become.

The enemy of your soul uses intimidation as a weapon to keep you paralyzed. He keeps a steady stream of propaganda— doubt, fear, and impossibilities—directed at your thought life.[1] If he can keep you focused not on what you do best, but on what you are afraid to do next, he has you. You will shrink back from your assignment and yield your dreams to doubt and uncertainty.

Your internal sound track plays a running commentary of comparison to others. You might see other people as being farther along than you are, happier, more successful, having more influence, more competent, more capable, more gifted … all the while diminishing the greatness deposited in you by God Himself. Too often this leads to regret, disappointment, bitterness, and jealousy. Instead of being able to celebrate the success of others, you may find yourself saying things like, "Must be nice …" and wondering why you don't have the same advantages—access to connections, resources, and "breaks" as others do. It is easy to minimize your accomplishments when they do not seem to be as large or significant as someone else's.

Your internal sound track is shaped not only by your thoughts, but also by the comments of others. Every dialogue buries itself in your subconscious mind. The sum total of all these thoughts and influences makes up your self-image. What you believe about yourself is of paramount importance.

Your internal dialogue shapes your perception of yourself and the way you interact with the world around you. It is imperative that you become self-aware and take control of the script. Practicing intentional awareness allows you to harness the power of your self-talk and use it to reach your highest potential.

You must know what God says about you. You must spend time with Him, meditating on His Word, listening to His voice, and knowing that His plans for you are good.[2] You must determine what you believe about yourself. You must take your thoughts captive and filter them through your passion and purpose. Conflicting messages can easily produce confused perspectives. This is particularly true when your self-image is at stake. What you say and believe about yourself determines how you project yourself through your words, your demeanor, and your communication style.

If your self-talk is positive, affirming, and encouraging, you will project a positive, upbeat persona. When you remain aware of your emotional state, you can access heaven's creativity and resourcefulness to meet any challenge.

However, if your sound track is negative, you will present yourself to others as pessimistic and cynical. You will look at problems as obstacles instead of opportunities, and your

WHAT YOU SAY AND BELIEVE ABOUT YOURSELF DETERMINES HOW YOU PROJECT YOURSELF TOWARD OTHERS.

mind will play out worst case scenarios. Your creativity and resourcefulness will be stifled by fear of lack, fear of failure, or fear of criticism. It is important for you to become aware of your internal dialogue so you can shape it. It is with you to stay. It is up to you to become intentional with your script.

How do you do this when you have little control over the things people say about you? From the time you were small your mind recorded everything said in your presence, taking in every word, logging experiences, and tying them to emotions. Sometimes it is hard to discern the difference between what someone else has said about you and what you have said about yourself. Make no mistake, your self-image is rooted in the internal voice you hear.

You only believe what you hear inside your own head. What other people say to you (or about you) is irrelevant unless and until you repeat it to yourself and agree. You can block negative thoughts and replace them with positive ones. You must choose whether or not to believe anything that has been said to you or about you. Become aware. Choose what you allow to "stick" in your mind. Good or bad, these things seep into your soul. You will rehearse them and soon the practice of your mind will become your reality. Your thoughts will become your actions. Your actions will become your habits, and your habits will move you toward or away from your destiny.

CREATED IN HIS IMAGE

You were created in the image of God.[3] Your original design is flawless. Along the way, negative experiences, negative emotions, and negative conversations have squeezed that image into something other than the original design. It takes an intense intentional effort to move beyond a negative self-image. Having a healthy, positive self-image does not happen by accident. It requires you to intentionally protect and preserve God's blueprint for your life. You must learn to pay attention to positive patterns and honor your victories large and small. Clothe yourself in humility.[4] Honor the image of God reflected in your life. When you feel unworthy or not equal to the task before you, cast your anxiety on Him and trust that He cares for you.[5]

Be self-controlled and alert. Resist the enemy when he attacks your mind. Stand firm in your faith[6] and speak positive words over your destiny. The tongue has the power of life and death.[7] This isn't true only of the words you say out loud, but of all the words you say—even those in your subconscious mind.

Your self-image is determined by choice, not chance. It is, after all, the expression of who you choose to believe yourself to be. Who you are, how you act, and how you interact with others, is a direct reflection of the person you have become. I am not suggesting "fake

YOUR SELF-IMAGE IS DETERMINED BY CHOICE, NOT CHANCE.

it 'til you make it." Pretending to be something you are not is disingenuous. But shrinking away from who you were designed to be is dishonorable. Instead, become intentionally aware of who, how, and why God created you to be. Align your thought life with His reality. Allow His Spirit to reveal His thoughts about you.[8] When you have the mind of Christ, your ability to influence the world around you will multiply. Get in touch with your authentic self—God's original design—before it was clogged by the expectations and limitations of others. You will experience a fullness you have never before known.

CHOOSE YOUR RESPONSE

What is your response to a bitter disappointment? What happens when something challenges your ability to believe in yourself? What frustrates you? Angers you? Intentional awareness is recognition that a setback or failure is not a permanent result. Whatever you choose to become intimate with will produce offspring. Courting betrayal, bitterness, and failure will cause you to reproduce these things in your life. Courting creativity, imagination, and victory will reproduce these things in your life. What "thought" children are you feeding? What are you nursing and supplying strength to?

Everyone has setbacks. No one wins all the time. But the most successful people see setbacks as challenges, not as failures. In fact, I celebrate even the darkest parts of my story. Those times when I was plunged to my lowest—abandoned, forgotten, and betrayed—served me well. I embraced the pain and sent my roots deep into God's Word. My character was challenged at every level. I wrestled with my flesh, I wrangled with principalities, and I activated God's promises in my situation. When I finally emerged from the fire and flood, I had been refined. I had the fragrance of Christ surrounding my life. He gave me beauty for ashes and in His time, through no manipulation of my own, He plucked me out of the pit, freed me from prison, and set me in a place where my life could bless others.

Failure is a part of the story. Falling down is a necessary component of developing balance. No infant has every learned how to walk without their fair share of falling down. Failure becomes a tool for growth when you engage in a process to move forward. Success is constructed out of the debris of failure.

I once heard of an experiment where an artificial habitat was created. A controlled environment was fashioned to provide optimal levels of temperature, moisture, and sunlight for plant life to flourish. All sorts of vegetation were planted with astounding results. Lush, rich growth flourished at an accelerated pace. However, as the trees began to stretch tall, something unexpected happened. They toppled over. One day a tree would stand upright and glorious, and the next day it would just tip over and fall to the ground. Why? The habitat was not programmed for adversity—storms. While optimal levels of sunlight and moisture were duplicated, there was no severe weather.

There were no rough winds, no drought conditions, no lightning, no floods. All the things that cause trees to send their roots down deep, find firm footing in the soil, and grow toward underground sources of water and nourishment had been eliminated. Without weather cycles to buffet the trees, their roots spread shallow and could not support the weight of the branches as the visible trunk of the tree rose tall and proud.

"Character is like a tree and reputation like a shadow.
The shadow is what we think of it, the tree is the real thing."
Abraham Lincoln

We are a lot like trees. A great deal of our strength lies beneath the surface—in places where no one can see. The glory is shown in the beautiful branches and luxurious leaves, but the real story is the root system that spreads far and deep—unseen, unsung, and absolutely vital to the health of the tree. If we focus all our growth on what is visible, we have little strength. A tree without a well-developed root system cannot provide shade or fruit for anyone.

IF WE FOCUS ALL OUR GROWTH ON WHAT IS VISIBLE, WE HAVE LITTLE STRENGTH.

CHANGE ATMOSPHERES

You have the ability to change the atmosphere around you. I suggest you also have the **responsibility** to shape the atmosphere around you. Being self-aware means you are engaged with yourself. Are you irritable? What's the cause? Is there a real problem, or did you just skip breakfast?

Are you fearful? What is creating your anxiety? Is there a real threat, or is your thought life running away with worst case scenarios? Are you in a good mood? A bad mood? Why? Self-awareness allows you to be in touch with your emotional state of being and understand why you feel the way you do. This empowers you to adjust negative circumstances and maximize positive ones.

Recently I was standing in a long line at the Post Office. There were only two clerks available to serve more than twenty people with packages and special requests. The mood was surly. The postal employees kept their heads down and served one person at a time, refusing even to make eye contact or acknowledge the long, long line waiting. Customers were tense. A few muttered under their breath, others made sighing noises, repeatedly checking their watches, shuffling from one foot to the other, and letting the world know they were annoyed. I was also frustrated. Standing in line was not what I wanted to do with my time. I had a choice to make. Either I impact this atmosphere, or I allow this atmosphere to impact me.

I tapped into heaven's resourcefulness and notified my face that a cheerful countenance was in order. I purposely struck up a pleasant conversation with the stranger in line next to me. I helped a mom struggling with restless toddlers. Then I cracked a joke about government efficiency and laughter broke the tension. We were all still in a bad situation, that had not changed—but now we were all in it together. There was a tangible shift in the atmosphere. People began talking to each other and swapping "longest line" stories. Someone let the mom with the toddlers to the head of the line. The charity spilled over and an elderly lady with a walker was given the same courtesy. Soon the clerks were smiling and engaging with a friendly, "May I help who's next, please?"

This didn't change the world, but it did influence my little corner of it that afternoon. This is intentional awareness at work. You have the power to shift atmospheres. It is up to you whether or not you will exercise that power.

Intentional awareness is also being sensitive to what others are going through. Everyone has a story. Maybe that rude waiter is dealing with a deep emotional challenge. Maybe the "too strict" teacher is up to her eyeballs in crushing debt. Perhaps the inconsiderate teen you just encountered has not heard the words "I love you" from a parent in months. Being aware that other people are dealing with things you cannot understand helps you engage them with compassion. You are called to be salt and light everywhere you go—not just to the nice people.[9]

INTENTIONAL AFFIRMATION

Affirming others is one of the best ways to use (and expand) your influence. You carry inside of you the power to elevate and lift. When you notice something about another person and take the time to mention it, you make their day. You esteem them more highly than yourself.

Something as simple as clicking "like" on a facebook status can bring encouragement. It shows you noticed what they had to say and found it compelling enough to respond. Telling someone they have a beautiful smile—and meaning it—can elevate their self esteem. Pausing to acknowledge the power of an expressed thought or comment can underline a person's value and create a sense of significance or belonging. Becoming aware of other people and recognizing their gifts and talents honors the Creator inside of them. Walking over people, devaluing them, or ignoring them altogether neglects your calling to encourage and build others up.[10] Your purpose is centered around people. God's assignment for your life is established in touching people. He is all about people. He created families, tribes, and nations. If you have problems serving people, you are going to have problems serving God.

PRACTICING INTENTIONAL AWARENESS PUTS YOU ON THE ALERT TO SEE GOD AT WORK IN THE LIVES OF OTHERS.

Practicing intentional awareness puts you on the alert to see God at work in the lives of others. It means you notice them. You pay attention to what they say and what they do. You encourage them. You lift them up, elevate them, acknowledge and praise them, and above all, you show them honor.[11] This pleases God and the harvest of affirmation you receive back will overwhelm you, "good measure, pressed down, shaken together and running over"[12]—I promise!

Awareness will only take you so far. In the next chapter we will look at intentional development. If you want to grow, you must learn what you do not know. Taking responsibility for your personal growth and development is fundamental to living with intentionality.

Endnotes

1. 2 Corinthians 10:3-7.

2. Jeremiah 29:11, Romans 8:28-39.

3. Genesis 1:27.

4. 1 Peter 5:5.

5. 1 Peter 5:6-7.

6. 1 Peter 5:8.

7. Proverbs 18:21.

8. 1 Corinthians 2:9-16.

9. Matthew 5:13-16.

10. 1 Thessalonians 5:11.

11. Romans 12:10.

12. Luke 6:38.

CHAPTER SEVEN

INTENTIONAL DEVELOPMENT

OF WISDOM ... OF CHARACTER ... OF SKILLS

There is untamed beauty in this world, the result of growth without restraint. There is also chaos. The wildness of nature produces a kind of magnificence that stirs the heart and inspires the mind. From the soaring peaks of the highest mountains to the blazing heat of the world's deserts, one is obliged to be amazed at the grandeur. The vast array of flora and fauna, the extensive and incredibly diverse assortment of fish, fowl, and every other animal form cries out for admiration. The grand design of God evident in nature compels us to worship.

There is a grand design. There is a Designer who brought it all together—from the most minute reaches of our planet to the vast expanse of the universe. Into that design, God introduced you—with intelligence, creativity, passion, and dexterity. No other creature remotely compares to you. You were created in the image of the Designer, created with the ability to do what no other creature on the planet can do. It is a gift of unimaginable opportunity and it belongs to you.

So, here is the challenge you face. Will you develop your gifts to their fullest capacity? Or, will you settle for living instinctively—content to wade through life without consciously embracing the myriad opportunities and challenges you face?

As you grow from infancy to adulthood, the changes you go through are nothing short of miraculous. But once you achieve physical maturity, what then? Will you continue to develop? More importantly, will you develop intentionally ... develop on purpose?

Life is a journey more than it is a destination. There is always more knowledge to gain and greater wisdom to embrace. There are new skills to master and character qualities to improve. Will you settle for attending the "school of hard knocks," or will you be more purposeful in your development?

Intentional development can best be defined as assessing and accepting the discipline and training necessary to become a better you—in your home, in your workplace, and in your world. A better you has greater wisdom as you exercise prudence and manage risk. A better you has a greater degree of personal integrity and moral excellence because of the intentional choices you make. A better you takes on the responsibility of learning new skills, techniques, and methods for accomplishing the difficult challenges you will face.

I ask you to consider these three areas on the road to becoming a more intentional person. The first is your wisdom; the second is your character; and the third is your skills. Each directly affects the way you relate to other people and your ability to complete your assignment. They are distinctly connected to your faith. Your worship, your expressions of service to others, your compassion, and even your loyalty are affected by your wisdom, your character, and your skills.

WISDOM

Wisdom has been described as the ability to see life's circumstances from God's point of view. It is the ability to use sound judgment, reasonable forethought, and keen perception. Every day of your life presents you with opportunities and challenges. Some are small segments of a busy day, where a well-chosen word or gesture can have a huge impact on someone or something. Others are huge, life-changing in scope. These require you to step back, breathe deeply, and cry out to God for His wisdom.

Most situations you face in the course of a day are common processes that happen again and again, testing your determination and requiring your strength. With these, it is easy to overlook the necessity of developing and embracing intentional wisdom. Experience kicks you into auto-pilot—"been there, done that." You respond by instinct rather than by choice.

As you develop the wisdom of intent, your mind filters through the choices you can make automatically and those you must consider thoughtfully. Though you have processed them a hundred times, wisdom triggers something intangible. This needs a moment! It needs consideration. Before you respond or react, wisdom causes you to stop and evaluate. Is this the same, or is it different?

Intentional wisdom is developed through experience. It is also developed through study and application.[1] As you deepen the well of your knowledge and understanding, you begin to recognize those threads of truth that make you better. Then, you apply them to your daily experiences. How you see and respond to life will be affected by the wisdom you develop. To pursue it only on impulse will have a limited effect. Intentionally developing your inner well-spring of wisdom allows you to exhibit that wisdom and walk within its boundaries.

HOW YOU SEE AND RESPOND TO LIFE WILL BE AFFECTED BY THE WISDOM YOU DEVELOP.

CHARACTER

Character is another part of who you are, a most significant part. Your character is a combination of your personality, your ethical and moral boundaries, and your personal integrity. For instance, we speak of people as being humble, or generous, or gracious. None of these qualities fully encompass a person's character, but they carry the implications of all that is required for someone to be just that. We may also describe someone as being mean-spirited, self-centered, or just plain evil. Again, these are merely one or two word descriptions of character, when in fact much more is involved.

Your character is multi-dimensional, a whole with many parts. Specific character attributes should be cultivated. While personality is an expression of how you approach life circumstances, character is an expression of what values and qualities you bring to life circumstances.

I encourage you to use some of the profile systems available with specific areas of focus. They are designed to help you evaluate and understand the dynamics of how you approach life. From the outgoing to the introverted, and from the calculated to the free spirit, your personality is fairly fixed. Understanding how you relate to others and how they relate to you is tremendously beneficial, but it in no way defines character.

I believe through heightened awareness we can learn to adapt our personalities and communication styles to be more effective in our interaction. Personality traits come with inherent strengths and weaknesses which can be addressed and adjusted. Learning how to blend your style with the personality styles of others allows for better relationships, mutual understanding, and the ability to have your needs met while you consider the needs of others.

Character, however, can change. Weak character can be strengthened. A lack of integrity can be reversed. This requires an intentional effort across time—the development of habits which embrace moral excellence, reliability, elevated ethics, and trustworthiness. People want to do business with those they can trust to be honest and dependable. They enjoy being engaged with you when they know you are authentic.

As a Christian, you carry a high standard of moral excellence as well. When people know you are a believer in Jesus Christ, they expect your character to reflect the values taught within the faith.[2] When you don't, you damage the image of Christianity across the board. You hinder the cause of Christ.

Taking an introspective evaluation from time to time is a healthy strategy for maintaining the excellence of your character. Have you dealt honestly with others? Sometimes we don't. Have you been unreasonably critical, or carried a negative attitude? Have you taken unfair advantage of a friend, a customer, or a family member?

Developing your character is a life-long endeavor. The world around you is filled with those who violate ethical excellence. People can be dishonest. They can swindle and deceive. The biblical standards of morality are widely ignored, and it takes great determination not to yield to the appeal the world offers—it is easier. Giving in to what everyone else is doing falls far short of being intentional about developing your character in a godly way. You alone can make the decision regarding what your character will reflect.

Every character quality you possess is because of choices you make. If you are honest, it is because you choose not to lie. If you are not honest, it is not an accident of nature. Treating people with compassion and kindness is a choice. Living within your means is also a choice. Everything you do, from how you care for your family to how reliable you are in your employment, is a result of a continuous list of choices you make. These are not written in a book; they are engraved on your life.[3] People read them and respond to what they read.

EVERY CHARACTER QUALITY YOU POSSESS IS BECAUSE OF CHOICES YOU MAKE.

People sometimes communicate they have one set of values, but live by a completely different standard. Such contradictions cannot be hidden. People know you for what you really are, not for what you say you are. Abraham Lincoln said, "You can fool all the people some of the time, and some of the people all the time, but you cannot fool all the people all the time." Your actions will prove the reliability of your words.

Unless you intentionally maintain your character, a kind of entropy sets in. Your character will deteriorate. Social and emotional forces are at work to draw you into lowered expectations of yourself. It is much easier to curse the darkness than it is to find a match and light a candle.

At the bottom line, character is actually a reflection of a person's relationship with God. When that relationship is strong and there is closeness between you and your Maker,

CHARACTER IS A REFLECTION OF A PERSON'S RELATIONSHIP WITH GOD.

you find that proximity to Him is power. His presence energizes your intentionality to develop your most significant self. If, however, that relationship is challenged, or non-existent, the converse is true. You will not have Him as a source of power in or influence over your life. You will be left to pull yourself up by your own efforts—an incredibly difficult challenge.

As for me, I want to live in a manner that is consistent with the character of the One who made me and makes His habitation in my heart!

SKILLS

I want my labor to be pleasing to God. When you commit the work of your hands to the Lord, work becomes worship. God created us with a need to be engaged in productive labor.[4]

In the Garden of Eden, where everything to sustain life was provided in a perfect environment, God assigned work to the man He had created. He made Adam the garden keeper. Adam had the responsibility to husband the garden and all the inhabitants within it. Man was never intended not to work.

Productive work is responsible for every invention and innovation that has been developed since the beginning of time. From the simple wheel and axle, to the inclined plane, to intricate nano-technology, human effort has been responsible for the advancement and development of practically everything. Nothing has ever been invented or created by a creature other than man. It is what God created man to do.

So, there you are—a creative, innovative, inventive replica of the original model, modified by sin and separated by thousands of years. Your abilities are a result of the investment you made of your time and energy to learn the skills you possess. Whether you are a welder or a brain surgeon, you have a specific set of skills you learned. You were taught by instructors and learned by experience.

The development of skills is required to fulfill your destiny. Early in life, I was aware I had a purpose. My parents spoke to me in the language of destiny and design. I knew my assignment was linked to lifting others. I knew I was placed on this earth to help other people see and activate their gifts. God equipped me with incredible creativity along with the natural ability to articulate ideas and harness ingenuity. I have studied literature and language, music and art, graphic

81

design, human behavior, leadership, and marketing. Only God could take that eclectic set of interests and blend it into a career that fully activates my assignment and allows me to help other people launch their dreams. Not one bit of my education and experience is wasted. All the components converge to fulfill my unique destiny—and yours will too.

Most of us do not set out on a clear course from childhood. Most of us have our lives unfold bit by bit. Circumstances and situations push and pull us, sweeping us along in life's current without planned direction. Each new twist reveals another step, moving us into another season where God challenges us to embrace His plan. Times of transition can be painful. Sometimes it feels as though purpose is lost and precious years have been wasted pursuing the wrong things. Let me encourage you— no time spent in preparation is wasted. Perhaps your journey to destiny has been delayed, but it is never too late to course correct and move toward an unlimited future. Even small changes, when made purposefully, can yield dramatic results. Don't give up.

NO TIME SPENT IN PREPARATION IS WASTED. DON'T GIVE UP.

Each new challenge you face and every new opportunity that comes your way reveals the necessity of development. Mastery is in the DNA of God. Sharpening your arrow, honing your sword, and gaining the edge are at the heartbeat of intentional development. Not only do you need to be clear about your assignment, you must invest in yourself to develop the mastery required to complete with excellence the work you are called to do.

Learning is a life-long process. Expanding your knowledge, mastering your skill set, learning and accepting new techniques and strategies is vital to staying fresh, current, and engaged. You simply must be intentional about continually developing your competence, your confidence, and your character.

You must master your choices, govern your faith, and control your emotional state as you reach for your destiny. No one has greater control over the outcome of your life than you. God has entrusted you with the gift of His image. You have language, creativity, innovation, and invention. You have perception and can work in collaboration with other creative individuals. You are productive, taking the resources of the earth and forming them into something greater, something useful to the betterment of mankind. You can use your ingenuity and wisdom to help others solve problems, discover new opportunities, and improve their living. You can build, form, foster, and shape incredible machines that reduce effort and increase efficiency. You can design systems and introduce strategies that free people from debt, protect their marriages, and empower their children. You can do anything that fits within the framework of your destiny ... if you master yourself.

Relentlessly pursue mastery and you will soon see the results as new opportunities unfold before you. In the next chapter, we will discuss intentional faith. We know that faith without works is dead,[5] but works without faith is hollow. Intentional faith directs our efforts in harmony and cooperation with God's plan.

Endnotes

1. Proverbs 4:7-9.
2. Matthew 5:16.
3. Proverbs 3:3-4.
4. Genesis 9:7; Ezekiel 36:8-11.
5. James 2:20.

INTENTIONAL FAITH

"The fundamental fact of existence is that this trust in God,
this faith, is the firm foundation under everything that makes
life worth living. It's our handle on what we can't see."
Hebrews 11:1 The MESSAGE

Between the fear of failure and the horizon of imminent victory lies intentional faith. Faith rises as the determining factor to press you beyond apprehension, beyond intimidation, beyond discouragement—to reach for the goals you have established and the dream you dare to dream. Intentional faith drives you to invest yourself in achieving your purpose. You are not bound by any station in life. It does not matter where you came from, how much money you have, or who has connections you don't have.

You have an unlimited future that is yet to be written based on the choices you make every day.

Invention is driven by the belief that something will work. The inventor *knows* it will work; he just has to figure out *how*. Thomas Edison knew, deep within himself, that he could create a device that would produce artificial light. Again and again he tried, using different materials and methods. Over and over, he was unsuccessful in achieving his goal. Did he give up? No. In the face of his disappointment and ridicule over years of unsuccessful attempts, he said, "I have not failed. I have just found 10,000 ways that won't work." His faith in the outcome caused him to persevere. I find great inspiration in Edison's perspective. He was a man filled with intentionality. He believed. He knew without wavering that he could accomplish what he had set his mind to.

FAITH IN THE OUTCOME WILL CAUSE YOU TO PERSEVERE.

Albert Einstein was one of the greatest mathematical minds the world has known, yet he failed arithmetic in school. When questioned about his brilliant discoveries, he said, "It's not that I'm so smart, it's just that I stay with problems longer."

Many people give up right before their breakthrough. When all that remains is one more push, they give in and quit. Faith gives you the strength to push one more time, the courage to try again, and the hope you will succeed.

GREATER WORKS

You have the ability to do something greater than you have yet done. Right now might be your time to do something brilliant. Something you will build, someone you will mentor, some idea or insight you have may well be the seed that grows into a cultural revolution. Do you know the name of Billy Graham's Sunday School teacher? Have you ever read about George Washington Carver's stepfather? Probably not, but their contribution paved the way for greatness that would change the world.

Our attention is too focused on the visible (or famous) contribution of others. Significant contribution is often overlooked and undervalued. Yet functioning within your calling paves the way for a chain of events beyond anything you can possibly imagine. Like a pebble tossed in a pond, the impact of your influence ripples out in ever-widening circles until it is felt on the other side of the shore. The point of impact may be all you notice. Do not judge its merit by how much splash is created, because in your wake you might be changing the shape of the surface well beyond what you can see.

Business revolves around innovation. Families grow stronger when parents learn to lovingly challenge their children and each other to greatness. Science fiction becomes science as ideas turn into prototypes. There are not enough hours in the day for you to sit and pine away about your inadequacies, your lack of resources, or your inability to create or execute a strategy. If you are going to become engaged in something greater, you must act. Belief demands response. Faith needs works.[1]

Life's pressures are great. Responsibilities can weigh us down. Just as the stress of gravity's pull makes life on earth possible, a certain level of stress is required to keep you getting up in the morning and moving forward. Survival in a sea of economic uncertainty, raising children in a culture of moral decline, maintaining health in a society wrapped in processed foods and entertainment overload is not easy. When in survival mode, it is difficult to deal with more than what absolutely must be done today. Feeling stuck in circumstances beyond control, it is easier to tread water and let tomorrow be nothing more than a carbon copy of today. *"If I can just get through this day ... if I can only make it until the weekend ... maybe next month will get better ...."*

It is easy to feel trapped, wishing things were different or better, but not believing they will be without a miracle intervention like winning the lottery or receiving an unexpected inheritance. We become like hamsters in a wheel, running, running, running ... but never getting anywhere. This does not need to be you. If you have gotten this far reading this book, then you are tired of being tired. You believe there is more for you. You know that God's purpose is greater than you have yet experienced. You are ready to surge into the future with fresh insight, renewed vigor, and a vitalized determination. You are ready to add intentionality to your faith and do something greater with your future.

Jesus said, *"Verily, verily, I say unto you, He that believeth on me, the works that I do shall he do also; and **greater works than these shall he do**; because I go to my Father."*[2]

Greater works! The same ability Jesus had to access heaven's resources to accomplish the Father's will is available to you. You can tap into the supernatural to accomplish even the most ordinary things. You have an edge. You have the power of God inside of you. He is an expert on every subject. There is no problem He cannot solve, no situation in which He cannot provide a favorable outcome. You can summon the unseen realm and activate the force of God's favor, the wisdom of heaven, and the perspective of eternity. How can you lose?

The transformation I have witnessed in my life is nothing short of miraculous. True, there was frustration and pain. There were errors in judgment and false starts. There were broken promises by people I trusted and disappointments when success was not as close as I expected. When I look back, I can see the hand of God at work in my life—every part of my life. Even when things did not make sense, I believed God's hand held me. I knew that nothing could touch me that had not first been filtered through His love and purpose. My faith was unwavering. This gave me hope no matter how difficult the trial I faced. I remained steadfast in worship and served the cause of Christ.

I KNEW NOTHING COULD TOUCH ME THAT HAD NOT FIRST BEEN FILTERED THROUGH GOD'S LOVE AND PURPOSE.

I tuned in to the Holy Spirit as a guiding strength for my life and trained my ear to hear His still, small whisper. I believed enough in His destiny for my life that I invested time, money, and education for a future I could only believe for.

To step into your assignment requires you to activate an intentional faith. It is more direct and purposeful than a general belief in God and His goodness. It is the ability to take up the shield of faith and block every dart of the evil one. It is the ability to stand, and having done all, to stand.[3]

Jesus responded to His Father by proceeding with an intentionality to fulfill His purpose. He never lost focus—never fell short of believing in Himself and His ability to achieve what He was sent to do. When He was challenged to give in and take a short-cut in the process, He cried out to His Father for strength. He remained faithful to the Father's will.[4]

While greater works in the Scripture obviously refers to things related to the Christian experience, I cannot overlook the fact that my work is completely connected to my Christian experience. I cannot separate what I do from who I am—from *Whose* I am. I am His, and everything I do is an extension of who I am in Him. What I am able to accomplish today is far greater than anything I have ever done before. For me, it is important not to lose faith in God, in myself, or in my destiny. Any time the dream feels like it is within my grasp, I go to God and ask Him to show me more. I need to know that my success is possible *only* with God. If I can achieve it on my own I'm not thinking big enough. When I get discouraged because something I have seen or believed seems too far off or too hard, then my faithfulness to remain engaged, stand on God's promises, and walk in obedience is evidence of the reality of my faith. My tenacity to persevere demonstrates the intentionality of my faith.

BURN THE SHIPS

Hernando Cortez was a Spanish explorer who helped conquer Cuba for the Spanish empire in 1511. When Mexico was discovered in 1518, Cortez set sail with a band of men and equipment to colonize the newly found territory, landing on April 21, 1519 near what today is Veracruz. In order to prevent all thought of retreat by his men, he burned his ships.[5]

In 2006 we moved our family from Georgia to Texas. It was a great leap of faith. My husband, Todd, left his position as a research technician with benefits and a 401(k). I left the security and fulfillment of full-time ministry and we stepped into an untried destiny as entrepreneurs. We didn't make the decision lightly. We clearly heard the voice of God and had received undeniable confirmation that our decision was the right one. We sold our home, moved everything we owned across the country, and leaped into developing the business. We "burned the ships."

The transition for our family had to work. There was no going back. I remember the early days when there was not enough business to keep the doors open. We would literally get dressed, go into the office, and pray for the phones to ring.

On more than one occasion, we ordered raw materials to create products when there was not one order present. Each time we did this, when the materials arrived, a customer call would come in to place an order. Our response time was lightning fast because we had materials on hand, and our reputation grew. Like Edison, we *knew* this would work—we just had to keep trying until we figured out *how*.

The historical record of the conquest of Mexico is an amazing story, filled with intrigue, deceit, vicious fighting, and merciless massacres. But with an initial army of less the 600 men, Cortez eventually conquered both the Mayan and the Aztec empires. His determination and commitment to claim the territory for the Spanish crown never wavered. "Burn the ships!" was his strategy. As a result, his men were highly motivated to make their assignment work. This may well be a strategy for you.

TO PURSUE YOUR COURSE, THE PAST NEEDS TO BE BEYOND YOUR REACH.

In your determination to pursue the course your faith has set you on, the past needs to be beyond your reach. The Children of Israel got caught in the Wilderness looking back on the provisions of slavery with selective memory, pining over what had been lost instead of focusing on what was ahead. Security, even as a slave, seemed better than freedom requiring daily trust in the provision of God. Sometimes a safety net or fall-back option is a hook that keeps you from taking the courageous action required to succeed.

CONCRETE, MEASURABLE ACTIONS

Intentional faith is more than words. It does require declaration and standing on God's promises, but intentional faith is about taking concrete, measurable actions. It is one thing to have a great idea, vision, or dream. It is something entirely different to act on that dream, take a step of obedience, and move in the right direction to make it happen.

Faith is related to action. Sometimes we have little to go on beyond what we believe—what we have heard God say, and what we know in the depths of our being is true. We *know* we will succeed, because we have seen the future in our mind. Faith articulates the dream—gives language to the impossible.

When I work with clients, we frame their big picture together. We put words to the big ideas and articulate what the future will look like as a result of them accomplishing their mission and meeting objectives. We set goals as though we already had hard dates on the calendar to launch their product or idea. Once we have that big, crazy, audacious dream uttered, it immediately seems more tangible. Excitement builds. Creativity and resourcefulness are unleashed. "I wish" turns to "I will" and momentum develops. Sure, there are a lot of scary steps ahead. There are things required to reach the dream that current resources and connections do not make possible. But faith is stirred, and faith is powerful.

We work backwards from the big dream, creating a strategy and an action plan. We chart a course that has concrete, measurable goals associated with it. Then I encourage immediate action. I ask my clients for a step of faith. Register the URL, file paperwork for the corporation, hire a designer for the logo or product packaging, get a writing coach, enroll in a class ... SOMETHING that is an intentional step of obedience and faith toward the future they desire.

It will be step-by-step that gets you there. There will be moments of acceleration and moments of setback, but dreaming of the future while saying "someday" and "wouldn't it be nice" will not get the job done. Faith without works is dead![6] When you act, you release something powerful. You build momentum and you begin to see yourself in that future. Choices become clear when a destination is determined. It is contagious. Once you have taken one tangible step toward making the dream a reality, you want to take another, then another, then another ...

REHEARSE THE DREAM

I have a dream book. It is a large scrapbook filled with pictures of places I want to go, the house I want to build, office space I love. I have articles in there that inspired or challenged me. Sometimes I have even cut out a single word from a magazine that sparked my imagination. I have encouraging notes from friends and prophetic words in that book. What am I called to do? What is the scope of my influence? Where do I want to go? What do I want to accomplish in life? What amazing sites do

I want to see with my family? When I get deeply involved in the grind and the perseverance required to press through is making me weary, I pull out my dream book. I remind myself that there is reward for labor. I take time to revisit my dreams and rehearse the promises that have been spoken over my life. This strengthens me and provides powerful incentive when there seem to be more bills than paycheck, and tomorrow is filled with today's unfinished to-do list.

Rehearse your dream. Say it to yourself and to others. This activates your faith. You believe what you hear yourself declare. You act on what you believe. Keep your eye on the prize. Know that fulfilling your purpose is a process and worth the pain. Nothing is birthed without struggle. Remain intentional with your faith and trust that what God has said He will do ... He will do.

In the next chapter, we will consider intentional influence. Influence is perhaps one of the most important dividends of living an intentional life.

Endnotes

1. James 2:20.

2. John 14:12 (KJV, Emphasis added).

3. See Ephesians 6:12-18.

4. See Luke 22:41-42.

5. Retrieved from: http://library.thinkquest.org/J002678F/cortez.htm.

6. James 2:17 (NKJV).

FAITH ARTICULATES YOUR DREAM.

IT GIVES LANGUAGE TO THE IMPOSSIBLE.

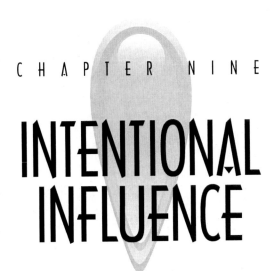

CHAPTER NINE

INTENTIONAL INFLUENCE

We all have people who influence our lives in one way or another. It could be because of their position, because of a personal relationship, or simply because we respect or admire them. These people cause us to think and help us make choices. We want to hear what they have to say and we emulate them. They have the ability to move us, inspire us, and challenge us. They help us toward our goals and the fulfillment of our dreams, even though they may be unaware of their influence.

You have the power of influence, too. We all do. Whether used positively or negatively, we all possess a measure of influence. Someone is paying attention to your words. Someone is impacted by your life and your choices. It is up to you whether this happens carelessly or you choose to become aware and use your influence intentionally.

Deep within you lie seeds of greatness—greatness not only for you, but for someone else. Perhaps your seeds will grow strong in many lives. Perhaps you'll be able to see some of them take root. It is wonderful when you can witness your influence touch someone else, but even when you do not know the true impact you make on someone's life, being intentional with your influence is worthwhile.

Words and actions you take to encourage, inspire, or motivate others are influencers. Careless words and actions that diminish or discourage others are also influencers. Whether or not you mean them to be, they are, and they have great power. Influence can be wielded as a destructive force, sometimes more easily than as a power of reinforcement and success. Why not use the power of your influence to strengthen and support someone else? The choice is up to you.

INFLUENCE IS A STEWARDSHIP

I look at influence as a stewardship. Influence has been granted to me in the lives of my family, my friends, my clients, and an ever-increasing circle of people I am privileged to touch. I am responsible to carefully steward the influence entrusted to me.

For some, influence becomes a commodity—that is, a possession to be used or misused. Once influence has expanded to significant strength, like you see with celebrities or in the political arena, it is often bought and sold. It is used to sell products or ideas with little regard to the consequences the influence wields. As a marketable commodity, influence is easily distorted, mishandled, and exploited. When used as a weapon instead of as a tool, influence can create considerable damage.

Your influence is (or should be) connected to the way God operates. It has the power to transform lives and promote people in a righteous, honorable manner. Influence is invested by empowering and encouraging others to grow and succeed. Like seeds that sprout into plants, influence can be planted and left to produce fruit on its own. As your influence mingles with that of others, it produces change and empowers people's hearts and lives. Ultimately, your influence can impact communities, regions, or even nations because of the compounding power of investment. Used in this way, you leverage your influence to expand God's kingdom on the earth!

When you fail to use your power of influence for good, it is wasted seed. Ask yourself why God would give you the power of influence if He did not intend for you to use it? God intends for you to use this power for His kingdom.

People listen to you. They seek out your opinion. They want your advice. That is power! Used for God's purposes, it is effective in transforming people's lives. Whether your influence brings them to faith, establishes confidence in their own abilities, or challenges them to attempt something greater and better, it is powerful.

Jesus' parable of the talents demonstrates this. The master gave three men different amounts of money to steward in his absence. Upon his return, he commended the stewards who increased the investment and condemned the one who did not.[1]

The point was clear. When you are given something to steward, the Master's intention is for you to invest it. If you protect what you are given to keep it safe, you are slothful and wicked. Even what you have been given to watch over will be taken away from you and given to someone who has embraced risk, and leveraged the asset for the Master's gain.

It is amazing how many lives you touch. Consider this. On average, we are approximately six people away from being introduced to any person on the planet. This is known as six degrees of separation.[2] The theory is that it is possible to have a friend … of a friend … of a friend … to six times removed, and be able to be introduced to every person on earth. Does that give you any sense of how widespread your influence might be? You simply do not know, and with the innovations technology has brought—the internet, social networking, and global communications—you swing a much wider loop than you realize.

You have a measure of influence with a number of people. Your experiences give you insight which blesses their lives. If you refuse to share your journey or withdraw into yourself, your influence has no capacity to touch others effectively. You must be faithful with what God has given you. If you aren't, the measure of influence you have will slip away and someone else will step in and venture it all to bring glory and multiplication to God's kingdom.

"He who is faithful in what is least is faithful also in much; and he who is unjust in what is least is unjust also in much."[3]

Your influence gives you a distinctive voice in a world of noise. As a Christian, you represent God and His kingdom. You must learn how to leverage your influence in a way that brings glory to God and provides others with the opportunity to change their lives.

CLOTHED IN HUMILITY

Humility is the awareness of God's grace in your life. Humility is an incubator for godly influence. The greatest influence possible results from mixing your obedience to God with humility. Recognizing the presence and power of God within aligns your purpose with your developed character. When you know who you belong to and you are submitted to His will, you recognize

HUMILITY IS AN INCUBATOR FOR GODLY INFLUENCE.

that influence is designed to lift others. Using the mastery of your skills and the power of your passion combined with humility allows you to assist others as they take the journey toward their better self. Thus, your unique giftedness carves out a powerful niche in the world around you.

No one else can be you. You must be the very best you possible. Your gifts and personality can only take you so far. At some point, you will be called to deliver on your promises— and you will need more than a warm smile and smooth words. Your gift and your personality, tempered by your character, bring you to the place where your influence broadens and its impact is enlarged.

ABUSE OF INFLUENCE

You can misuse your influence more easily than you might imagine. You can carelessly succumb to inner temptations that will derail you from walking in obedience to God. People with great potential sometimes stumble when promoted and find themselves in the glittering limelight of exposure. What begins with pure motives can easily become tarnished with self-inflated importance. Beneficial influence cries out for a humble spirit and godly character.

I have witnessed people make major life decisions—and major life mistakes—based on a casual, careless comment dropped across a table by an admired mentor. When influence increases, you must be very careful not to over-extend your measure and harm or manipulate others. It is exciting to be asked for advice, even when you are ill-equipped to address a subject intelligently. Draw on the wisdom of God, always. He is an expert on every subject, but never be afraid to give an honest, "I don't know." People trust you. Honor their trust.

There are many ways in which influence is manipulated and thus destroys the benefit it brings. Making something sound like Scripture and using it to underscore a message is offering spin, not truth. Unfamiliarity with Scripture has caused more than a few people to twist the truth to support an impressive point they are trying to get across. Usurping or siphoning off another person's authority to add to your own measure is both immoral and deceitful. Using your gifts to draw attention to yourself is prideful and pretentious. Assuming authority or power that has not been delegated or released to you is seditious and disloyal to those you should be submitted to.

All of these things are violations of God's purpose for your influence, and you should intentionally avoid them.

MAXIMIZING YOUR INFLUENCE

"You are the salt of the earth; but if the salt loses its flavor, how shall it be seasoned? It is then good for nothing but to be thrown out and trampled underfoot by men. You are the light of the world. A city that is set on a hill cannot be hidden."[4]

The challenge is to use your influence in a righteous way. Jesus compared the lives of His followers to salt and light. Salt is both a flavor enhancer and a preservative. It makes things taste much better and it slows down the process of decay. Light illuminates. It dispels shadows and reveals distortions. Broken places can be seen. Hidden pathways can be followed.

Both salt and light influence the environment around them while not being at opposition with them. They have no fight, no sense of struggle or competition. Rather, they enhance their surroundings by bringing flavor and clarity.

You were crafted to have influence, fashioned in a unique way to enhance the lives of those around you. While not everyone with whom you come into contact will respond openly or favorably to you, your influence will touch many people.

YOU WERE CRAFTED TO HAVE INFLUENCE, FASHIONED TO ENHANCE THE LIVES OF THOSE AROUND YOU.

Your influence determines how well you are able to lead people, encourage them, or challenge them to reach for higher productivity, efficiency, and opportunity. Your influence can motivate people to rise above their circumstances. Many have become dissatisfied or disappointed in how they live. They need someone like you—someone who loves them without an agenda, someone who cares about them because God loves them, someone who delights in their victories, and celebrates their success.

I have learned to pay attention to how my life affects others. I listen to their comments. I value their feedback. I take notice of their words of appreciation or concern. I am encouraged when someone communicates how my life has blessed theirs. I am intentional about how my influence touches people because I am intentional about my relationship with Jesus Christ.

I am filled with gratitude that God trusts me to touch His children. I am honored to be a vessel through which His anointing can flow. It amazes me. It humbles me. But if I was not intentional about stewarding my influence, I would totally overlook its importance and move on with my life. If I focus inwardly I will not touch others with greater purpose.

I invite you to become consciously aware of your influence. Regardless of how large or small you feel your circle may be, you should use your influence intentionally to bless others. Significance is not measured by volume. Here are some suggestions that have helped me steward what God has given me. I am confident they will help you, too.

1. **Become intentional about your assignment from God— your ministry and mission.** Jesus left us with the understanding that we are to continue to do business while we wait for His return.[5] Expand your business. Build your skill set. Strengthen your character, and focus on your purpose. Being consciously consistent with God's agenda for your life is the pathway to success, and success is an open door to influencing others. People look to those who are successfully accomplishing their goals and achieving excellence in their field for insight and wisdom. So be faithful with the work God has called you to do.

2. **Learn to walk in obedience to God's Word**. Scripture provides the best and most effective path to being successful. The world around us is overrun by people with compromised morality, a lack of ethical stability, and self-seeking motives. Marginalized integrity is an easy option, but it's a slippery slope. For those who would intentionally invest their influence with a kingdom view, there is no room for compromise. Even in small things, God is the one who orchestrates our opportunities.

"Grow in the grace and knowledge of our Lord and Savior Jesus Christ."[6] Read, study, and meditate on Scripture. Becoming mature in your faith is a direct result of being familiar with God and His Word. As you learn to talk with Him and listen to His voice, you will become more and more mature.

3. **Maintain proper motivation.** Do not give in to manipulating your influence to get ahead or position yourself for an advantage. My friend Jan Greenwood says, "Use your influence under His influence." Listen to the Holy Spirit when He directs you and encourages you to show interest in someone else. Righteousness requires right motives, right attitudes, and right actions. It is difficult to have a beneficial influence on others when your attitude toward them is sour or your actions toward them are insincere or without real integrity.

4. **Use your influence to glorify God.** Press forward His interests, His strength, and His power. By bringing others into the awareness of His presence, you give them the

freedom to experience what only He can give. In the process, you have the blessing of being a part of His plan, working to establish His love in the hearts of those you touch. You encourage them with His wisdom, challenge them with His honor, and love them with His love.

5. **Reach beyond your borders.** It is important to expand your influence beyond the walls of your church, your home, or your immediate circle. Christians are notorious for their tendency to cloister themselves together and resist outsiders. This is not the way to leverage your influence, or to expand God's kingdom. Jesus walked among people who were far removed from His character and insight. He touched them with love and compassion. He intentionally poured out His best for their advancement. Influence should be used to inspire and motivate, not condemn or bring judgment. Love large!

6. **Eliminate negative influences in your life.** Just as you are an influencer in the lives of others, others are influencing you. Sometimes, it becomes necessary to withdraw from individuals who exercise a negative influence over you. Do they discourage you from your dreams? Do they limit you? Hinder your efforts? Hold you down? Do their words bring life or death to your spirit? Friend or family or foe, no matter, if their influence is toxic in your life, you need to remove yourself from their reach. Nothing will serve to diminish your influence quite so much as being manipulated or controlled by the negative influence of

someone else. Necessary endings are an essential ingredient to practicing intentional influence.

Napoleon Hill said, "Think twice before you speak, because your words and influence will plant the seed of either success or failure in the mind of another." This side of heaven, you will never truly be able to measure the scope of your influence. Guard it well. Become a faithful steward and learn to direct your influence with intentionality.

Endnotes

1. Matthew 25:15-30 (NKJV).

2. **Six degrees of separation** refers to the idea that everyone is on average approximately six steps away, by way of introduction, from any other person on earth, so that a chain of " a friend of a friend" statements can be made, on average, to connect any two people in six steps or fewer. Retrieved from: http://wikipedia.org/wiki/six_degrees_of_separation.

3. Luke 16:10 (NJKV).

4. Matthew 5:13-16 (NKJV).

5. Luke 19:13 (KJV).

6. 2 Peter 3:18 (NKJV).

LIVE WITH PURPPOSE...ON PURPOSE!

Intentionality is meaningless without purpose. Passion is a driving force, an inner engine of delight in doing the things you do. Lack of passion has relegated men with unbridled creativity and skill to poverty. Others have ample riches, but lack of passion leaves them without any genuine sense of accomplishment or contentment. In between the two extremes are those who live life without much thought to their purpose or being part of something greater than themselves. Living paycheck to paycheck, distracted only by entertainment and leisure, they find their fulfillment as spectators, vicariously identified with the achievements of others.

You, on the other hand, have decided that living without being fully alive makes no sense whatsoever. You recognize there is more. You want more. The only thing holding you back … is you!

Choose to become intentional with your life, and you will quickly see the impact of your choices. If you will thoughtfully approach your passion and tap into the core of who you are, discover how you are wired and what makes you tick, then you can begin to find clarity regarding your purpose—your assignment. The more you focus your natural gifts and skills toward your purpose, the greater joy you will experience in your everyday life. Your influence will increase. Your ful-fillment will expand, and you will begin to see how you connect with others in the beautiful mosaic that makes up the big picture.

Everything in life has purpose. There are no coincidences. Mistakes serve to help us grow and learn. If you will turn down the ambient noise in your life and get in touch with yourself, you will have the opportunity to craft your destiny, rewrite your own script, and step into your unlimited future.

For me, providing for the success of others has been at the top of my list. That has been the engine that powers my career in the motivational arts, personal and corporate branding, and publication. Everything I do as an entrepreneur has a component of my passion buried deeply within it. When I am engaged in my assignment, work is not a chore. It is a delight. I am energized and empowered, full of insight, and surrounded by acquired wisdom. I have the pleasure of using my gifts, skills, and personality in ways that advance others and fill up my destiny. When I cannot do those things I become lethargic and weary. Dark clouds of frustration and gloom creep in. That is when my intentionality kicks in—my determination to press through the darkness, back into the radiance of my passion and purpose.

Many people have never made the effort to define and understand their purpose. Not fully aware of their passion— the *why* that propels them—they often pursue careers based on financial prospects, parental suggestions, pressure from peers, or just expediency. Vainly they search for purpose, perhaps deciding on some meaningful conclusion, only to discover there lies within it no real sense of fulfillment. Thus their sense of purpose is artificial, a supposition without intensity. A lack of real purpose leaves them without much vision. They drift through life, living—but never fully alive. Very few, once they have become entrenched in a vocation they don't enjoy or appreciate, extricate themselves and pursue something that would light their fire. That is sad, because it is never too late.

Learn to live on purpose. I say learn, because it does not happen automatically. Becoming intentional with your words, your thoughts, and your actions requires a great deal of awareness. You function on auto-pilot far more than you might think!

Being shy or having a driven personality is no excuse for being unaware of your purpose. Living with intentionality forces you to keep close account of the details of your life. In essence, intentionality is a stewardship over your emotions, your thoughts, your words, and your deeds.

Is your passion being fed? Is your faith strong? Is your purpose being fulfilled? Are you making progress toward your goals? Are you setting new goals after you reach those? Are you making wise choices and expanding the effectiveness of your influence? Answering these questions honestly and thoughtfully empowers you to view them with intentionality and direct your course in cooperation with your destiny.

Grab hold of your passion and come alive. Come fully alive. Stride confidently into your purpose and embrace it with intentionality. Live with purpose ... on purpose!

MEET THE AUTHOR

Wendy K. Walters has a gift for identifying what makes a person unique and bringing that to the forefront. Like few others, she can guide you through the maze of distinctions that make you stand out—looking better and sharper, maximizing your originality. As a consultant she has helped launch many people's dreams, translating their ideas into profitable businesses.

Author of several books including *Marketing Your Mind, Selling Without Sleaze—Marketing With a Conscience,* and *Postworthy—Words to Encourage and Inspire.* Wendy has also developed a powerful *Brand Profile* that recognizes core competencies, pinpoints core values, identifies the problems you are uniquely gifted to solve, and helps target your niche market, and develop your signature brand.

As a partner in Palm Tree Productions, Wendy not only coaches people through the process of developing intellectual property, she has the resources available to bring those ideas across the finish line into tangible reality—creating products and platforms for services.

She speaks at conferences and business events, activating and empowering people to declare their dreams, identify with their passion, and create strategic action plans. Wendy points others confidently toward their destiny and encourages them to walk each day with intentionality—living with purpose, on purpose! She finds no greater joy than seeing others released into their potential and living 100% fully alive.

www.wendykwalters.com

Marketing Your Mind is written in three parts: Branding Yourself, Writing Your Book, and Marketing Your Media. Drawing from her experience both as a branding consultant and as a partner in Palm Tree Productions, Wendy offers you a practical, simple guide to developing your intellectual property and turning your ideas into marketable media.

The *Brand Profile* is an assessment tool created to take you through a process of discovery to identify your "unique factor" and pull out your core competencies, core values, developed skill sets, and areas of mastery. It helps evaluate your intellectual property to target your market and develop a signature brand. Wendy uses this tool with her clients and has now made it available for personal use.

Selling Without Sleaze—Marketing With a Conscience unites biblical principles and common sense. Intended for those who feel uneasy about marketing themselves or placing a value on their services, Wendy shows you how to confidently market what you have to offer without selling your soul.

Available at:

w w w . w e n d y k w a l t e r s . c o m

Speaker | Author | Consultant